AUTOBIOGRAPHY OF A

MURDERER

Hugh Collins was born in 1951 and grew up in Glasgow. He served
sixteen years of a life sentence in prisons round Scotland, including
the Special Unit at Barlinnie. He was released in 1993 and now
lives in Edinburgh with his wife, the painter Caroline McNairn.

D1437765

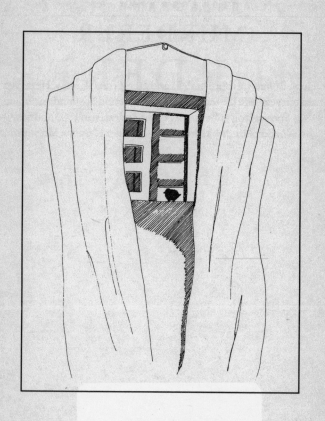

AUTOBIOGRAPHY OF A

MURDERER

Hugh Collins

PAN BOOKS

First published 1997 by Macmillan

This edition published 1998 by Pan Books
an imprint of Macmillan Publishers Ltd
25 Eccleston Place, London SW1W 9NF
and Basingstoke

Associated companies throughout the world

ISBN 0 330 34978 3

1 3 5 7 9 8 6 4 2

A CIP catalogue record for this book is available from
the British Library.

Typeset by SetSystems Ltd, Saffron Walden, Essex
Printed by Mackays of Chatham plc, Chatham, Kent

To my wife, Caroline McNairn.
Also to the memory of my grannie, Auld Cathie Collins.

ACKNOWLEDGEMENTS

Without the fundamental principles of justice which underlie a democratic society I would most likely now be dead. I have come to respect these principles and the many people who defend them against those who would undermine them for short-term political gain. I am now released under licence for the rest of my life. I have someone somewhere to thank for signing the release papers and giving me a second chance of life. I hope this book pays tribute to the many people who showed fairness, understanding and good will – it wasn't an easy task. They include my mother, Betty Norrie, my brother Alec and step-father, Jim, my closest friend, Linda McNee, my wife, Caroline, and her family, Andy and Lorraine Arnott, Andrew Brown for his faith in our friendship, Malky McKenzie, Jimmy Boyle and Larry Winters.

This book would never have been written without Bill Buford. Also Robyn Marsack, many thanks. For their courage in publishing the book I thank Peter Straus and Catherine Hurley. Finally, William Mooney: I would rather that he were alive today than the existence of this book.

PROLOGUE

I **FIRST BEGAN** writing some fifteen years ago in my previous life: my previous life in prison. In the time it takes to pass through a doorway I had been metamorphosed. In a flash what had been my life had become my past: 5,840 days; that's 140,160 hours forgotten in a single moment. In the 50,457,600th second it ended. Name and number, arsehole!

What I had left of it was on paper. Yes, I wrote about it while I was in there: wrote about it day after day, month after month, year after year, all sixteen of them. The diary dictated and I took notes: it demanded that I observe and record. The diary became the master, depriving me of indulgence, denying my every whim. I became the observer, observing the observed, never quite reaching it, never quite getting there, always that step behind, always in the past, stalking the present. That's the thing about writing – you can never quite get to that point, that one singular moment we know as the present, because by the time you get there you are already in the past.

Now, the present is telling me that I have to take the past, relive the past, if you like, but live it, as it were, in the present. I don't know if you get this. I don't know if it makes sense.

What I'm going to do now is write about all that, write about the past while living in the past, pretending to be in the present. Will I ever catch up? Will I ever get there in time?

I get the feeling that I'm looking back into space, looking back at the past, at the velocity of light travelling across the universe, at stars that have already imploded, collapsed in on themselves. I get the feeling that this is the shape of time, that time is the reflection of action.

So who then is it writing this book?

Time, that's who: time is the past, the past pretending to be the present. The dying present pretending to be the future, the dead author pretending to be alive – me.

Who am I? Who was I?
Hugh Collins, Collie, Shug, Hughie – the common denominator. Caucasian male, born of William Collins and Betty Norrie Collins on 17 June 1951.

Height?
Five feet ten inches.

Weight?
Eleven stone.

Build?
Muscular.

Hair?
Grey-brown.

Eyes?
Grey.

Vision?
A slight astigmatism. Corrective lense required for reading and watching television.

Tattoos?
A tattoo the length and width of my back, consisting of a

network of concentric circles and different-coloured stars – the result of an acid trip in prison.

Other distinguishing characteristics?

Scars. From the bottom up. One the shape of a W on my calf: from a gang fight with the Tongs when I was fifteen, a member of the Shamrocks. Twelve stitches.

Two scars on my back. The first is about an inch to the left of my spine. After I was arrested for murder, and while awaiting trial, I tried to escape. My plan was to become so 'ill' I'd be moved to the Royal Infirmary. I got a friend to ram a sliver of mirror into my back but, in his enthusiasm, he pushed it both too far in and too close to the spine.

The second is on the right, higher up. Another gang fight with the Tongs. I was eighteen. I was stabbed with a bayonet and slashed across the length of my back with a car aerial. Eight stitches and a long hairline scar from the car aerial.

One on my hand from the day that Wee Joe, a schoolfriend, tried to pin my hand to a table with a carving knife.

A scar on my forearm, the right one, from Saughton Prison, when I tried to break up a fight.

The head?

About five on my scalp, mainly from the police. One is from a steel bar – from when I was beaten up in prison by William Mooney, the man I later killed. Also a scar behind my right ear from a fight with Wee Joe in 1971.

And the face?

Principally the seven-inch scar along my jawline, continuing up behind the ear. Nobody fails to notice it: shop detectives single me out, children ask me if it still hurts, civilized people at dinner parties stare at it when they think I'm not looking.

How did it happen?

I was surprised by a butcher's cleaver. Ninety stitches. I

believe the intention had been to kill me and that the target had been the jugular. They missed.

In prison a psychiatrist suggested that I have plastic surgery – that, unless removed, like the scars on my father's face, it would mean that people would always respond to me as a violent man. An operation was arranged but on the day I changed my mind: the scar is me, and to remove it would be to deny who I am, deny my whole life.

CHAPTER ONE

I'M FIVE AND A half years old, attending St Roch Primary School in Glasgow. The teacher, Miss O'Donnell, has asked us each to stand, walk to the front of the class, and tell the others what our fathers do.

'My da's a railway worker,' says one, and sits down.

'My da's a postman. He delivers the mail.'

It's my turn, and I walk to the front with some pride. 'My da,' I say, 'is Wullie Collins. He's like Robin Hood. He takes from the rich and gives to the poor. My da's a bank robber.'

The class erupts, shrieking with laughter. I'm immediately embarrassed. Miss O'Donnell is taken by surprise. That's the end of that exercise, and my granny is summoned.

'He's not a bank robber, Hughie. You mustn't say that. You mustn't ever say that.'

So who had told me?

Did I get the idea from Ginger McBride? Once we get past the confusing stage in which it was maintained that my father was in the RAF, there are regular visits from men who have been with him in Peterhead Prison. They tell us how Wullie runs the prison; how all the screws are scared of him; that he won't speak to them, even to give them the time of day; that he's the boss. They always bring something, a wee present for Wullie Collins's only son. Tony Smith, the skinny man with a nose hooked like a claw hammer, brings me a woven Celtic scarf. He is younger than my da, but one of his best pals (Skinny's brother, Granny tells me one night after Skinny has left us, was hanged for murder), Gypsy Winning is another. Gypsy is tall – six foot two – he tells us stories, too, towering over my granny and me. When he comes, he brings me a toy gun. And then there is Ginger McBride.

I'm sure, in fact, that it was Ginger who said that my da was the Robin Hood of Scotland, a bank robber who helped the poor. The last time he was here Ginger McBride brought me a knife. The knife is very heavy and has a tartan handle and a long, thick blade like a dagger. It is my first knife.

My first memory is not of my da – I know him only by the pictures my granny shows me: it's of my ma on a cold, wet night. I can't be more than two years old and am wrapped in a blanket and held in her arms. We're walking fast, looking into deserted buildings. I remember the gaslights and the dark shadows. I'm crying for some reason, maybe because of the dark and empty streets. She's crying, unable to find the address she's looking for and needing a place for us to sleep. We spent the night in a room in a deserted tenement, huddling together on the floorboards, her coat around us.

At some point – I don't remember when – we go to live at my Granny Collins's house on the Royston Road. Granny Collins has a large family – there's Jack, Shug, Charlie, Cathie and Alex, who is only eighteen months older than me – and now I'm to live with them. I don't remember my mother going. I look for her and she's gone.

I learn later that my mother's parents were against her marrying my father. Wullie Collins was a troublemaker and always in fights. My mother's father, Bob Norrie, a Clyde shipyard worker and lecturer for the Socialist Party, a conscientious objector during the war, wasn't going to have Wullie

Collins in the house. His wife was a devout Catholic, his complete opposite, and yet they were devoted to each other and never had an argument in their married life. But they wouldn't take my mother in that night, not even with a small child.

As a boy, though, I used to go to see my grandfather on Sunday afternoons, and he'd lecture me on physics and astronomy and scientific socialism, rewarding me with half a crown when I caught on to what he was saying. We did mental arithmetic, too. I became fast at that, but it led to my first experience of the belt. One of my teachers couldn't see how I'd arrived at an answer to a mathematical problem without pages of work and accused me of copying the answer from another boy. He ordered me to stand in front of the class and attempted to belt my hands. I was a child, not John Wayne, and the very thought of that belt terrified me to the point of pissing my trousers. The teacher had a practical method of dealing with such reactions: he simply seated you next to a wee lassie who continually wet herself, and was considered the class dunce: she was his personal punch-bag and object of ridicule. The teachers at that school were absolute bastards, without exception; every one of them took pleasure in inflicting pain and humiliation.

The night my mother and I slept on bare boards was the night my father was sent to prison. It wasn't for bank robbery; it was for a razor slashing. The judge, one Lord Charmont, was determined to make an example of my father, a deterrent to other slashers. Until then, no sentence had been longer than two years: usually no one did time at all for slashing. But it had become a Glasgow epidemic and my father, having slashed the manager of the Locarno dance hall, was given ten years. The dance-hall manager got nine stitches. Ten years for nine stitches: that's thirteen months and ten days for each stitch. Everyone tells me it isn't right; everyone who comes with stories and presents says it isn't right. Much later, in prison myself for a slashing, I will hunt out the newspaper clippings and trace my father's fame, taping them to the wall, staring at them. His name and his picture were in all the papers.

I don't know this man, the father I've never lived with, but I feel a powerful loyalty to him. Where do they come from, feelings like these – so strong, yet based on so little? I have no experience of being his son, yet I want to look after him, defend him, protect him from justice. And I want him to look after me, to teach me things, everything: how to be like him. I want to be a son he can be proud of. When my mother takes up with another man while my father is still in jail, I explode with rage at the terrible unfairness of it all. Years later, unforgiving, I call her a whore (and then hate myself afterwards for saying it).

Another picture. I am eight years old, asleep and in the same cot as Alex. I think of him as my brother, although he's really my uncle. Granny is shaking Alex by the shoulders. She is fully dressed and crying. 'Wake up, Alex,' she says. 'Wake up. Yer father's just died.'

My grandfather had worked on the railways. The suit he got married in was what he wore to work; it was the only one he ever had. It was blue serge, a three-piece suit. He wore big tackety boots, a wee scarf tied round his neck – they all wore those, it was like a uniform – and a bunnit, a cap. He was always covered in oil, but I don't recall his ever having a bath. You would see him at night with his long johns on, and he had a huge semmit (vest) which he'd tie underneath, like a nappy, and you'd see him running to the bathroom, totally bald, with his false teeth. It was comical, really. He'd come in at about ten o'clock at night, drunk, and sit in one of the chairs for a few minutes without saying a word, chain-smoking Woodbines. Then he'd go into the bedroom and you could hear him spitting. He had a bucket by the bed and I had to wash it out in the mornings.

For days everyone is crying. I cry, too, although I'm not sure why. I don't think I understand what has happened, but I'm infected by the sadness.

I remember that several days later the children – me, Alex and Cathy – find ourselves alone in a room with Grandad. He is in a coffin. We poke his face and the skin is cold and tough like a football. Someone finds some lipstick. What would Grandad look like with red lips? Alex is giggling as I rub great gobs of the stuff across Grandad's face. 'He's like Coco the Clown,' I say, and everyone laughs uncontrollably.

It's when we arrive at the funeral that I see my da. He's been let out of prison to see his father buried. I've seen him before, behind a plate-glass window, dressed in blue and smiling at me. He's different now. He doesn't acknowledge me, his only son. He doesn't acknowledge anyone. Wullie Collins is dressed in black: a long, immaculate black overcoat, a black suit, shiny black shoes, a black tie and steel handcuffs. He is surrounded by four screws and stands by the grave, silent. Everyone around him – the family, friends – is weeping. My father is still. His face, covered with scars, doesn't reveal a thing. I study the face and will remember it for ever: it is hard, like a stone. Wullie, the hard man, people say. Yes, my da, the hard man.

CHAPTER TWO

I **DON'T THINK MY** family could have changed anything. Perhaps if one of them had had enough insight to see what was lying ahead, and had told me the truth about things . . . The wildness was just part of playing in the streets, like all the boys. If I'd been told the truth, could I have been rescued? I'd have felt sorry for my da, of course; as it was, no one ever came out and said that what he'd done was wrong. He was my granny's eldest son, and she tolerated all his behaviour.

When the parish priest visited, he didn't say anything either. I was quite a shy wee boy and I'd hide behind Alex when he came. It was like God coming into the house. When I was an altar boy, standing in the chapel, with the smell of incense and candles and the paintings on the walls, I had no difficulty in believing that God had done the paintings. God lived in the tabernacle, didn't he? One day I was there with Alex and I decided I'd have a look inside. 'There's nothing there, Alex! God isn't there!'

It sort of broke a dream. I remember I used to sing all the hymns. One Christmas Eve I had joined the cadets and we were singing away at mass, with our uniforms on, but I saw the women giggling and I got self-conscious.

I believed in God and fairy tales, all the things weans believe in, but I think my da's being released smashed all that. He was a very violent man with a terrible temper, not the hero from my childhood.

I was eight years old when he hit me for playing with a boy from the same street, Brian McQueen.

Most boys played cowboys and Indians: they had sticks with a flattened tin on the end as makeshift tomahawks or a piece of wood for a rifle. But Brian didn't play those games – he played doctors and nurses, or houses, lassies' games. He spent time with the lassies and he liked Cliff Richard. One day I was dressed up in Cathie's jewellery. I had a skirt on and high heels, and I was covered in lipstick, playing at the front of the close with Brian. Two taxis drew up, and out stepped my father. There were six or seven other guys with him. He was walking right by me when I said, 'Da!'

He looked at me. 'You get up the fuckin' stairs!' he said, and slapped me on the back of the head. 'Don't ever let me fuckin' see you dressed up like that again.'

That was the only time he ever struck me.

He was just out, having served six and a half years of his ten-year prison sentence in Peterhead. Somebody took me to Peterhead when I was very young. I remember seeing my da: at that time he was in a black uniform with a blue-and-white striped shirt, huge eyes, a very handsome man with black, curly hair. In the barren visiting room there was a photograph of an aeroplane on the wall and a prison officer in uniform. So I could believe my mother's tales of my da being a pilot in the RAF.

● Years later, in the Special Unit, there was an arts festival and the Chief Prison Officer of Barlinnie, Rocky Frazer, was invited. He was a big, tough-looking screw who had fought a lot of square-goes with prisoners. He was chatting with my mother, Jimmy Boyle and Ken Murray.

'Do ye no remember me?' said Rocky Frazer.

My mother was laughing. I knew who he was, but didn't know what he meant.

'I used tae make yer bottle in Peterhead.'

'That's right,' my mother said. 'He used to take you in to see your da behind the visiting screen.' This was when I used to be stuffed with tobacco, all inside my shawl. 'Right, Wullie, ye can haud him,' said Frazer; my father would extract the tobacco and put it inside his jacket.

'Aye, I used tae make yer bottle,' repeated Frazer.

'Well,' I said, 'fuck knows whit ye were puttin' in it 'cos ah'v never been out the jail since then.'

There were a few screws there who'd been in Peterhead with my da, and some of them were quite friendly towards me. Once I'd been in Larch Grove (a juvenile remand centre), where you wore short brown corduroy trousers and a brown jersey, and where there was always fighting. I'd turned a dining table over and thrown bowls around, a juvenile tantrum, so I was sent to Barlinnie as being unruly. I was absolutely petrified. I must have looked like a wee lassie walking into the prison hall. There were people there from the age of sixteen to sixty – it was the 'untried' hall. They put me in a cell.

A big screw opened the door. 'Are you Wullie Collins's boy?' he asked.

Right away I brightened up, thinking it was a friendly face. He looked like Santa Claus. I said, 'Aye, aye.'

'Well, ye'd better behave yersel' in here, ye hear?' he said, and slammed the door. I was shattered. I don't know what I expected from the guy.

When my da visited the unit he always blanked the screws. He wouldn't say a word to them when they were trying to communicate. There was just one exception, Walter Davidson, who had worked in the surgery at Peterhead. (He'd been a bastard in the traditional system, but he was brilliant in the Special Unit: he really got caught up in it. One day I found him out cold in my cell and thought he might have had a heart attack. I went rushing off to Jimmy Boyle and said I hadn't touched him. Jimmy came with me and shook Wattie awake. It became an incident we talked about: a Chief Officer could fall asleep in a cell without being taken hostage. That was what the unit was about: building up trust.) My father was his passman – cleaner – in Peterhead.

Wattie came up to us one day in the Unit. 'Can I ask you something, Wullie? How did ye steal they pills?'

'We were emptying out the capsules and then putting the blanks in the bottles again,' said my da.

'That's it! We were issuing medication and it wasnae having any effect.'

They reminisced for about ten minutes, but that was all. The screws used to talk to the visitors when they escorted them up from the gate, and they became familiar with some of them. There was almost a family atmosphere – that was what Jimmy and I were working for. Such a structure was aimed at the Scottish Office, to show how things could work and ask why it wasn't attempted elsewhere. But my father insisted that I tell the screws not to talk to him.

A screw who'd been with him at Peterhead said to me once, 'You know, your father was a model prisoner.' He'd been friendly with the prison staff and other prisoners. That came as a surprise to me. I discovered that in his generation there were no staff assaults: they were quite shocked when men like me and Jimmy Boyle started battering screws. But didn't my da run things? Wasn't he the boss?

● The Beatles had come on the scene about the time my father got out of Peterhead. He bought us plastic Beatle wigs. I remember when my friend Jokey Costello came round one night; his mother had shaved his head because of nits, and he had this Beatle wig on for real. My father was in hysterics when he answered the door. He gave us both half a crown. He bought me a Beatle suit, too, made of mohair, which cost the astonishing sum of £18.00. When we went to the shop to get it, he said to me, 'If you're asked, the name is Wylie.' So it must have been a scam of some sort.

He'd sit and watch television with me on his knee, but he did things that really made me squirm. He asked, 'Whose legs d'ye like the best?' when we watched the chorus line on the London Palladium show and murmured, 'Look at the tits on that one!'

My da rarely stayed with us. One night when Cathie's boyfriend was round seeing her – he was quite a big guy, John, who didn't really get on with any of the family except Jacky – I was watching TV. He came in and switched over to the racing. My da came in later.

'I thought ye were watching that cowboy thing.'

'John turned it over,' I said.

My da switched back, and the atmosphere was really frightening.

'I was just watching the racing,' said John.

'But he wants to watch the cowboy film,' said my da.

John went out and slammed the door. My da jumped up. At that time he was very fit, before they stabbed him in the neck (now he walks with a terrible limp and can't use his arm).

'Who slammed that door?'

My granny answered. 'I think it was John Kilpatrick.'

My da ran out of the room. I went to the window with my granny, and we saw John flying out the close, and his face hit the bars where the railing had been removed during the war and caught on them. My da was kicking him. John never fought back – it was a horrible thing to see. I felt revulsion then: my father was a hero to me, and seeing the violence really frightened me. Then he came back up and got washed. It was as if nothing had happened.

Sometimes he'd come back with women and we'd hear noises from the end room.

When I was about thirteen a gang was shaping up, but it hadn't been declared a gang. My da told me that he had a house in Springburn and that I could come up with my pals and have parties and he wouldn't bother us. We thought he was great. The place was a shambles, just a drinking place for him and his pals. One night when we went they'd been having a wine party. There was a living-room with a wax cloth on the floor, a couch, a couple of chairs and a table laden with bottles. They were all four drunk. As we came in they were arguing. I didn't realize how men of that age fought: it was punch for punch. Harry Jasper punched my da. I picked up this old-fashioned iron, the kind with a heavy plate and no cord, and battered Harry with it. He lay there with his head all cut.

No one tried to stop me. In fact my da was quite chuffed that I'd done it. 'Aye, that's my boy,' he said. He was full of admiration.

There was a big streak of blood down the wall. Harry just lay there.

I said, 'I want to bring my pals up.'

'Aye, bring them up,' said my da, 'and we'll have a party.'

Then Harry sat up, covered in blood. 'Wullie, whit wis that all about? Whit happened to me?'

'That was my boy – he did that,' said my da.

● I'm very young, not yet at school. Somehow I can read words: the names of shops along the Garscube Road. My ma is asking me to read the letters: 'What does that say, Hughie?' We're on a bus. My mother has long, light-brown hair; she's beautiful and all her friends are nice. Someone always gives me a toy to play with: a fire engine, a yacht, a Davy Crockett hat. I have lots of toys and lots of clothes: red sandals, thick tartan socks, a greenish jumper. She makes me eat up all my food: we eat together at a table in a house.

● My mother wears a green coat; she has a leather bag with a clipping-machine strapped over her shoulder. I press the button – click, click, click. She's smiling at me, combing my hair, tickling my belly. I'm sitting on the coal bunker in the kitchen of my Granny Collins's house in Royston. Ma's home from work on the buses. Why does she go away?

Alex takes me out to play in the street. He tells his pals that I'm his wee brother. I love playing cowboys and Indians; sometimes we play at war and we're all soldiers. I miss my ma. Where has she gone? I only see her now and again. Where is she? I watch for her coming up the street. Sometimes I think I see her and cry when it's not her. When she does come, she brings toys and takes me to a café, buys me ice-cream. She lives in Cowboy Land, I tell my pals, on a big ranch with horses, and my da flies aeroplanes for the RAF, fighting the Germans. I read about him in war comics, and my ma drives the Deadwood stagecoach on television. She knows Davy Crockett. I tell my schoolfriends about my fictional parents.

I don't wait for my ma to come any more, but she still does, sometimes, with a man in a big car. She gives me money to buy sweets: I love buying sweets. Sometimes I buy a present for an old woman across the street, Mrs Fagin. My Granny Collins tells me to go for her messages because she can't walk; she's my granny's pal, so I do everything for her. I love my granny: she's my maw; my ma is my ma – there's a difference.

Alex and I play football every day after school, like all our pals. We play at every opportunity, two aside, twelve aside, anything just to play. At Christmas my maw gets us real football boots and annuals too: *The Victor, The Valiant, The Broons* and *Oor Wullie*. I love Christmas, staying up all night after midnight mass, finding our presents in the morning and going back to chapel for mass – it's a great time. We go swimming a lot: I have to wear my maw's knickers and they open up like parachutes when I dive into the water. Big Willie John Monaghan takes us all to the Campsie Hills in his van; he tells us stories about Rob Roy McGregor and my hero, William Wallace. I love my family and all my pals in the street; I love growing up with them; this is my whole life.

'Yer faither is in a jail, Hughie.' My maw is telling me

something, but I don't understand. It's because there's something in a newspaper.

Alex is telling me things about him too. 'Aye, Hughie! He's a great fighter, so he is. He robbed a bank, too, so he did.'

Wallop! Alex is clouted round the ear.

'Shut the hell up, ya swine ye are!'

My maw wants me to write to my da; he misses me, he's in Peterhead Prison. My poor da is in the jail, but he's a bank robber . . . Dear da . . .

● My ma comes to see me with that man again, in the big car. She tells me that I'm going to have a wee brother, but I have brothers already, don't I? They give me money. I don't want to be with her any more. I can buy sweets but I don't like her any more.

I'm growing up rapidly. My da is out of jail; my ma has a wee boy called Alec but he isn't my brother, I don't like him. My granda is dead, my maw is working her way towards it. I do cleaning jobs with her. My ma has a house near Royston; when I visit her every Sunday she gives me money. I don't know why, but I've lost all feeling for her. She didn't stand by my da, and she abandoned me, didn't she? The money's handy, though my da gives me more. He still loves her, he says, especially when he's drunk and sings songs all night about her. We seem like 'passing strangers' now. Funny how things can change.

● My ma is in tears.

'Hughie, for God's sake, son! What have you done?'

She has four prison officers behind her. I have four behind me. Two more are guarding the exit door. We are in the security visit room: there is a glass window and wire mesh between us. I'm caked in congealed blood, having stabbed three screws in Perth Prison. My ma heard the news on television and has demanded to see me. What can I say? 'I'm sorry?' It's too late: I'm totally fucked up.

I used to go to see her sometimes, when I wanted money, knowing that she couldn't knock me back; she was living with a guy who wanted shot of me.

Once she began to get at me when her mother was there. 'Hughie, you're starting your dad's carry-on . . .'

'Fuck off,' I said.

'That's your mother you're speaking to,' said Granny Norrie.

'My fucking mother's dead.'

I felt bad as soon as I came out with it, because I knew I'd got to the bone, and then I couldn't face her. I ran away from the relationship – and from my brother.

My ma visits me for sixteen whole years, almost every single visit she's allowed. During that time I discover things about my childhood, about the way she was squeezed out of my life. Why should I believe her? Even dead, my granny is my maw: how can I change my feelings now? My ma has constructed a whole history about us, whereas my da volunteers nothing. She's got drunk a few times with me and told me things I didn't want to hear, things about their relationship. Was I just a one-night stand up a close? I mean, there you are, thinking the whole world was waiting for you to arrive, and it's just not true.

Jimmy Boyle and the Special Unit bring us together; we build a relationship, but I'm resentful, feeling that it's too late. My ma persists, no matter how much I resist. I can't touch her physically, or my brother Alec: they don't know how difficult that is for me. To be held in their arms – it's too fucking late.

Jimmy pushes me all the time: build new relationships, express your feelings, learn to let go, be sincere and honest. What the fuck does he know? Fuck them all. My ma keeps on, supporting me through crisis after crisis. I don't like the place one bit; it drives me mad with its community meetings, crisis meetings, discussion groups, visitors and more visitors. I have no say here, no real power. Jimmy keeps telling me to confront situations, find out what happened, rebuild relationships. People talk about the healing powers of community. Just let go of your negativity, be constructive, be positive. Sounds great, doesn't it? Wave the wand! The prisoner is transformed; he's totally reformed, a new man, no problem. What's to be changed? I ask. What's there to heal? What's the point – to prove to society that I'm not an animal? I don't care what society thinks: I am a fucking animal. I enjoy violence, don't I? I liked stabbing screws, every moment of it. Who wouldn't?

● I set up a visit so that my ma was sitting there when my da walked in. I'd seen them together only twice in my life. He'd just finished his ten years and was living in a place down the bottom of our street. My granny sent me down and when I went in, the two of them were in bed, having spent a night together. I think they tried to get me into bed with them, but I ran away. Perhaps I was embarrassed. I hadn't grown up with that kind of thing – seeing parents naked together. I think I became quite puritanical about women. The last time was when they fought over me in the middle of the street. I'd been dragged from my bed in a blanket; they pulled me this way and that until finally my granny grabbed me. 'Get the hell out of here!'

I'm pouring tea all over the place, in a panic: my da is sitting quietly, overcome. I'm squirming with nerves, being so constructive. My ma can't believe that I've arranged a visit with both of them at the same time. Now I'm being positive: we're a family, aren't we? Surely we can develop together as adults, learn to trust our emotions, support each other? My ma's staring at me in total disbelief; my da's looking at the floor as I speak. He's squirming, too, listening to his boy talk this way, talking about relationships and our personal problems. We have to be positive about our relationship. Surely we can talk about it, can't we?

My ma bolts to Jimmy's cell. My da remarks that he's read about Jimmy in the papers. In terms of violence, I'm my own man: now he's sitting there wanting to rub shoulders with Jimmy and she's run away to Jimmy . . .

What the fuck am I doing? What am I trying to prove? My

ma is furious – can I blame her? My da hates the Unit and what it's trying to do to me; he could never have lived here, he says. Jimmy is just working his ticket, he says. My da likes walking up and down in the yard, and so do his pals; they like visiting and reminiscing about the old days. 'Here, Wullie, this is just like the jail, eh?'

My ma is enraged that he brings his pals to visit me and points out how contradictory he is: did he visit you before the Unit? Did his pals visit you then? Jimmy and Ken agree with her. She goes on: 'They make me sick.' She wants me to get a grip, pull myself together. She wants me to read socialist books, do my stone-carving and be creative. 'Hughie, try to be positive, son. Educate yourself while you're here. Look at Jimmy. That man's trying to do something for other people. You don't see him with every bampot on the street up visiting, do you?'

Kay Carmichael's a good friend, she says. 'Kay's fond of you, Ricky Demarco and Jane MacAllister too. These people care about you. Your da? Jesus Christ, Hughie, do you know what he said to me? When you were in Perth after that carry-on, and he's making excuses as usual about not writing to you, the usual crap about not having spectacles, but he can afford the drink. Well, anyway, he's going on about all the usual nonsense and then he comes away with this: "Betty," he says, "I think we've produced a monster."'

CHAPTER THREE

OF COURSE, WE WERE poor, but I wasn't very conscious of that. When Jimmy Boyle started talking about 'deprived areas' in the Special Unit, as though that explained everything, I said I wasn't deprived.

I wore shoes with cardboard inside them. We used to get the old comic annuals, with thick board covers, and sit by the fire to cut them up for inner soles. That stopped your socks flapping out – otherwise you'd walk up the road with your socks flapping and never think about it. Everybody was in the same boat.

There was plenty going on in our lives. Everyone played football in the street. I remember seeing Jack with his mates stepping out of the close, dressed to the nines in their mohair suits for the dancing, and they'd end up with their jackets off, sweating over a game in the street with us until dark.

We were totally unaware of the pressure on our mothers. I don't think they had a lot to share with us, emotionally, because all their energies went into survival. The women were absolutely dependent on their men for money, but they were allowed to do what they liked with it. In those days – in the 1950s – a woman on her own couldn't have had an independent existence. Other women would have shunned her and called her a whoormaister.

In fact, the men depended on the women in practical ways; they couldn't have coped on their own. If I'd gone to do the household shopping, as a young man, I would have been automatically put down as homosexual, a poof, a bent shot. Other men – or the women, if it came to that – wouldn't have allowed you to do the shopping.

The domestic scene was dominated by a woman until her husband appeared, drunk, on a Friday night. Every Friday night he was drunk. She could have whatever was left in his pocket. Or he would come in from work, give her a set amount, then be off to the pub. All the money would be spent over the weekend. On Sunday night I used to be sent out for single cigarettes – three Woodbines – and that was the money done.

I remember one time when my granny couldn't pay the rent. It was about £18, I think. She disappeared. We were all running about, and I wandered into the chapel – I was an altar boy then. I found her there, in tears. I was out stealing that night and got the rent money.

We broke into a shop at the bottom of the street. It was on the ground floor of a tenement that had been vacated and was about to be pulled down. We were in getting scrap metal, copper and lead pipes and somebody put his feet through the floorboards. So we dug a hole and put a board across, then let down a rope and emptied the place. We grafted all night. We hid the stuff in a coal cellar under Jokey Costello's house – we were as thick as thieves then. There was money, too, two bobs and half-a-crowns [10 pence and $12\frac{1}{2}$ pence in today's equivalents]: it came to about £50. We got boxes of chocolates with the money and went round the doors giving them to all the old women. And we had things like bottles of Dettol, and we'd go up to women saying we'd found them; they could have them for Christmas. Isn't that what my da would have done? We were planning to go to the pictures. I had about fifteen or twenty quid on me in this bag of silver; my pockets were bulging. And I ran into Charlie. He asked where I got it from. I was in tears, peed myself, was terrified to say that I'd broken into a shop. I said I'd found it.

'Right,' said Charlie, 'up the road.'

I got leathered and the money disappeared. I heard my granny say, 'That's the rent, then.'

It was really exciting, though, and we finished up by breaking into nearly every shop on the main road. It was very easy: the burglar alarms were connected to the doors, but we came in through the ceilings or the walls. Once we didn't notice the time and looked up and saw that it was light and people were standing at the bus stop outside the shop. We kicked open the doors and ran out, and the people rushed in, picking up bags of coal and things. My granny was there; I'll always remember her face when she saw me. I must have been about fourteen. By then she knew, I suspect, that I was out breaking into shops. Kids used to be allowed out on the streets till ten o'clock or so on the long summer nights; then you'd hear the women calling, 'Come up!', and they'd go in to bed. I'd say I was going round to Jokey's to play; his mother had boyfriends and was often away. Things would appear in the house – tins of food and things I'd put in the cupboard. So I think my granny knew, but there was no point in saying anything really, and also I was providing. I always had money, stealing from the rich to give to the poor. Just like my da and Robin Hood.

● For some reason Auld Cathie, my granny, had decided to keep me off school for a few days, and during this time she wasn't able to pay one of the debt collectors. There were four or five of those: the TV was on hire-purchase, there was insurance, and the money on goods from catalogues came to about seven shillings and sixpence [37$\frac{1}{2}$ pence] a week. I was told to say that she wasn't in, though she was there, hiding behind the door. The debt collector asked when she'd be back, and I stupidly turned round, saying, 'Maw, when will ye be in the hoose?'

Wallop!

I heard her apologizing as I landed in the toilet.

'Whit a wee swine that boy's gettin'! Did he tell ye Ah wisnae in?'

I always hated going to school anyway. The school janitor seemed to be in a permanent state of apoplexy, with his fat, red face and bulging eyes, always shouting. One day when he bawled at me I was scared out of my wits and ran from the school, my face covered in flecks of spittle and the smell of his boozy breath in my nostrils. I sat in a nearby swing-park, consoling myself with thoughts of flooding the toilets, wiping my nose on my sleeve, when Jokey Costello appeared. He was dogging school, and we kicked a stone around: it was great, feeling free!

'Shooey,' he said, 'let's play on the lifts o'er in the flats!'

The high flats on Royston Road had replaced the old tenements and had been considered posh with their electric fires and central heating; they had verandas where you could see right across the city. And they had lifts, which were a novelty and a favourite playground for kids.

'Aye, Jokey, it's a great idea. C'mon, then, pal!'

On the way, we came across an old van and, on pulling open the rear door, we discovered a heap of cardboard boxes containing packets of Indian tea, labelled 'Poonakandi'. We thought we had discovered gold! Immediately we began to fill our pockets with packets, although we had no idea what we were going to do with them; it was just pure devilment. Jokey found two old coal sacks; we stuffed them full, then went back and forth through the flats to a back court on the other side of the Royston Road. It was a real adventure: we filled a narrow passage in the back court with packets of 'Poonakandi'. We didn't notice the time go by until Royston Road was swarming with women getting in their messages.

Auld Cathie and Mrs Costello seemed to appear out of nowhere, swinging their shopping bags.

'Right! Ya swines ye's are! Get up that bloody road!'

My maw skelped me round the head with her bag and kicked me right up the arse as I ran through the close with Jokey.

'Wait tae Ah get you up that bloody road!'

When we looked back, we saw a crowd of women gathered around the front of the close where we had hidden the tea. It deepened our terror of going home: we decided to run away.

'Jokey! My ma's a cowboy wumin in Cowboy Land – we can go there!'

We hid in an old tenement house, and later that night we ripped up its floorboards and climbed down through the ceiling into the newsagent's below. Big John, the local beat policeman, discovered us there some time after midnight, pot-black and stuffing ourselves with cream cakes. When we were taken home in a police car, all the women were watching from their windows. Big John lectured me about my behaviour. 'Next time I'll kick yer arse fur ye.'

My maw scrubbed me with a floor scrubbing-brush in the sink but didn't leather me as I'd expected. She simply sent me to bed, saying, 'Nae mair nonsense, ma boy, or it's a home fur ye.'

A 'home' meant approved school, which terrified me. The thought of being taken away from my family was enough to change my behaviour, but I did notice that the whole street seemed to be drinking 'Poonakandi' tea . . .

I loved my maw. One night when we were all in bed we overheard an argument in the scullery. It was Cathie and John. My maw went in: we heard a slap, and my maw cursing: 'Ya big swine, ye!'

I leapt out of bed and grabbed the first thing that came to hand, a huge flower vase made of thick glass. John had his back to me as I ran into the lobby; glass flew everywhere as the vase burst over his head. I hit him as hard as I could. 'Don't hurt my maw, ya big bastard!'

Nothing was ever said about my action, but I later found out that it was actually my granny who had skelped John. Well, my da had battered him anyway, hadn't he?

*

● Even at primary school, Joe Devlin was big for his age and seemed to be in endless fights. Kids would rush up to the 'Coup' – the football parks behind the school – at the end of the day to watch the fights, forming huge circles round the opponents. Being Joe's pal had obvious advantages but also its risks, involving battles with children from the neighbouring Protestant schools. All I knew about our division was that while I was a Catholic altar boy, they were Orange bastards. Once, when I was playing in the football parks, I was hit by an older boy swinging a Boys' Brigade belt; there was a gash above my eye. The teacher who had been refereeing the football match chose to reprimand me and grabbed me by the scruff of the neck. Before he could haul me off for a belting, he was hit on the head by a half-brick, thrown by some spectator. Joe jumped on the teacher, punching and head-butting until he let go of me, and then we ran off.

I dodged school the next day, and the day after, scared of the repercussions. About two weeks went by, and during that time I was caught shoplifting pocket diaries and keyrings in a city store. When the police took me home, Auld Cathie was told to report to the station. There, a few days later, an inspector gave me an official reprimand and warned me that I was heading for approved school.

● Davy Bean and I were playing in the cabin of a coal lorry. I noticed what I thought were throat lozenges, wrapped in Cellophane. 'Look, Davy – sweeties!' We were away within seconds, the lozenges stuffed into my pocket. They turned out to be threepenny pieces, ten shillings' [50 pence] worth. We bought boxes of chocolates for all the old women in the street and a slug-gun. It was my first gun, with real bullets (pellets). I loved firing at pigeons, feeling the jolt as I pulled the trigger – *spoosh, spoosh, spoosh!*

A few days later, while hanging curtains for Auld Cathie, I looked down and saw the coalman looking up at me from his cabin. A few moments later I heard his voice, talking to my maw at our front door, and the words 'ten bob' . . .

Auld Cathie caught me with the sweeping brush, breaking it across my back as I tried to run past her. 'Ya fuckin' swine, ye!' I then took the biggest hiding of my life from her: 'Ya swine! That bloody man works hard!' She hit me with everything – a mop, belts, old wet cloths, anything she could get her hands on, and I learned one thing: never steal from your own kind.

● One night we were listening to records at some lassie's house and drinking cheap wine and cider. One of Jack's pals had to carry me home. He knocked on the door and bolted, leaving me swaying on the landing. When Auld Cathie opened the door I fell in, singing a sheltic shong. She couldn't believe her eyes: eleven years old and pissed out of its mind, singing Celtic songs. Jesus! Would ye credit this! She lifted me by the scruff of my neck and almost drowned me in cold water. The scullery was going round and round, and I finally vomited all over her apron.

'Aw, fur the luva God! Wait tae yer faither gets hame!'

I managed to keep clear of her for a couple of days, sheepishly creeping around, and the matter was forgotten, thanks to an incident involving the gasman. Like most of the women in the street, my maw had access to a home-made gas-meter key, which allowed them to borrow a few quid in shillings from time to time, replacing the money when their financial position improved. On this occasion the Gas Board van had appeared unexpectedly in the street, and kids could be seen running to the shops to get shillings for their mothers to put back in the meters.

'Hurry up, Maw. He's at our close!'

She put the coins in and carefully replaced the container just as there was a knock on our door. I was sitting on the coal bunker beneath the meter when the gasman came into the scullery.

'Dae ye want a wee cuppa tea, mister?'

'No, thanks, son.' He smiled. Then he burst out laughing as he slid out the container. 'Jesus! This is amazing, Missus Collins!'

My maw was mortified as we looked inside the container: there sat ten pounds in single shillings, evenly stacked in piles.

● Jacky had started work as an electrician. His obsession was Celtic. He and his pals used to go up to Barrowlands, dancing at the Palais. He was the first person to give me pocket money. I used to polish his shoes and try on his smart clothes, imitating him in the mirror. Alex got involved with me, breaking into places, and he became the leader of the gang. Jokey's elder brother, Arthur, refused point-blank to break into shops. He had a hare-lip and was very self-conscious about it – a nice man, very straight. His other brother, Tommy, was like a modern-day Fagin. He'd been to 'housey' – approved school – and we were awed by that. He was about sixteen, the same age as Jacky. He wore pointers and an army belt, which was a sign of being hard – so was a Boys' Brigade belt, both of them covered in studs. He also wore a bolero jacket with a belt at the back, and his hair hung down in front; he'd chew on a lock of it. He was the ultimate rebel, a Marlon Brando figure. He once forced Jokey and me to fight each other with heavy studded belts. Jokey was my best friend, yet Tommy forced us to leather each other until we were completely exhausted, with cuts all over from the leather catching on the bare skin. When Auld Cathie saw me, she came down and battered Tommy. She used to have a big floor cloth, which was always soaking, and she'd catch you round the neck with that and then *wallop*! She was a very powerful woman with huge arms; she'd swing you about all over the place.

She broke Tommy's hold over me, exploding the whole myth, but he kept on giving Jokey terrible beatings. For some reason, Alex then turned on me. He'd begun to see himself as a big fighter; everybody was fascinated by Cassius Clay at the time, and Alex began to shadow-box and beat me up. It would start as a carry-on, but if I retaliated he would hit hard.

One day I stuck a screwdriver in his back, quite far. He'd whacked me with a steel ruler, and I just flew at him. I must have been about twelve. Things were never the same afterwards.

CHAPTER FOUR

NOTHING SERIOUS happened until the year the Beatles brought out *Rubber Soul*. I began growing my hair then. My granny couldn't afford the gear when I began to take an interest in how I dressed, and in girls. But it was the long hair that the headmaster of St Roch Secondary School objected to, and he decided that I should be put in with the girls until I had it cut. So there I sat, day in, day out, all the local talent around me; I wasn't the least bit bothered. Joe was pleased, too, as I could pass on his love notes. After a while the headmaster couldn't stand it, and he had me up in front of the whole school. His remarks about my hair didn't upset me, but then he got more personal.

'So, Collins, do you wear girls' clothing when you get home?'

'Ya old bastard,' I muttered.

'Right, laddie, it's six of the best for you,' he said, whipping out what looked like an old poker.

That was enough for me, with the whole school there. I made a break for it, but he was too quick and blocked my escape. Being Joe's friend had its advantages: he'd shown me how to head-butt. I got the headmaster right on the nose, knocking him out cold, and then took off.

This made me someone special in everyone's eyes, even in Joe's, and I lapped up the fame.

I was expelled from school a year before I was due to leave, but I didn't dare tell my granny, so I had to fill in the day. I began to go to town, sitting for hours with a Coke in Woolworth's cafeteria. I met Albert Faulds that year. He had jet-black hair that he kept cropped short so that no one could grab it in a fight. He had just got out of approved school and, like me, was roaming about, looking for something to do. At one point we got proper jobs, working in a clothing factory. I'll never forget how I felt going home with a wage packet in my pocket. All the way home I kept asking people the time, just so that I could say, 'I'm on the way up the road from work – I want out early for a pint.' They gave me some funny looks but I didn't care: now I was a man.

Having spotted some material that I was convinced was mohair, and having clocked the fire escapes and alarms, I couldn't resist going back to the factory one Saturday night and making off with rolls of cloth. We sold it to friends and punters to make fashionable suits, but it turned out to be synthetic material, intended for suit linings, and as it stretched and sagged and came apart, more and more unhappy customers came looking for us.

That was the only job I held for years. Soon we were back at Woolworth's. Joe Devlin joined us: Joe was calling himself the Bear. He had always been big for his age at school so the nickname was appropriate. He brought Wee Joe Mulligan, and before we knew it we had the makings of a gang. We called ourselves the Shamrock, and eventually it had about fifty members. We were fifteen, and found a pub that would serve us: what a drink that first drink turned out to be. The next morning I swore not to touch another drop of the stuff, and for a while I didn't. The Bear and the others always wanted to hit the pubs, and I didn't want to be seen as a bampot, so I joined in sometimes. Then it was girls and dancing instead of drinking, but I really wanted to be with the gang, who'd started going over to the South Side, carrying their open razors.

The Shamrock members were all Catholic and all from the Garngad. People joined it for various reasons: some because it was a part of living in the area, a natural progression from being fanatical Celtic supporters; others because it gave them status – they had protection and gave loyalty. The more commitment an individual showed, the more respect he won. Commitment involved absolute loyalty to the gang, regardless of the consequences – and those were ultimately being killed or life imprisonment for murder. You could demonstrate commitment when outnumbered by another gang in a confrontation; you could retreat and lose face, or charge, ensuring respect and reinforcing your own gang's reputation for being game. The guys who ran away didn't last long anyway; someone would turn on them, and they'd be slashed or beaten up.

Albert, the Bear, Wee Joe and I were exceptional. We never ran from anyone; we all enjoyed fighting. We didn't join the gang: we *were* the gang. We didn't invent codes or rules, they tacitly emerged from our perception of what was game. That we'd grown up together greatly influenced the general pattern of the gang's conduct. To attack another gang member who may have become involved with a girl from our area was out of the question, and this developed into an unwritten rule concerning people who were not involved with gangs. There was nothing game about slashing someone out on their own or with a girlfriend. Certain things were taboo: hitting women, housebreaking, mugging, rape.

There were females in the gang, girls who would come along whenever we were going to fight a gang in another district. They carried our weapons in their bags, as the police had no power to search them. The girls had no say in matters, nor did we fight over them. Many simply had sex with almost everyone, some even gang-banged – it was just another aspect of gang culture.

One night they came up for me and asked me to go into town with them. Albert gave me a meat cleaver. When we got to George Square, the atmosphere there was electric. Everyone was on a high and ready for anything. The Bear, looking like a general, shouted, 'Head for the South Side! Go right ahead with any cunt you see!'

We moved off and nothing happened until a shout came out of nowhere, 'Cumbie, ya bass!'

Suddenly there were knives flashing all around me. A lunatic appeared in front of me and I kicked out but he stabbed me in the calf. I was lying there, helpless, while the crazy bastard tried to slash my face, when luckily for me the squeal went up: 'Bizzies!' I was carted off to the Royal Infirmary to get stitches in my leg. When my granny appeared I nearly collapsed with fright, but she was too worried to start on me.

These Glasgow women defended their kids with single-minded ferocity; they would fight in the streets if they felt their kids had been unfairly blamed for something. My granny believed the Shamrock to be a group of teenagers hanging out together in cafés; she had no idea of the extent of our activities. These women had no time to read the newspapers, which covered an increasing number of violent incidents and voiced concern over gang-warfare. My being stabbed reinforced my granny's belief in my innocence. Her son wouldn't slash or stab anyone; he was the victim of someone else's son.

After a few weeks in the house I was back into town with the boys, only this time I was armed to the teeth and looking for my assailant. It was a long time before we met up, and in the meantime I was getting more reckless every day: being stabbed hadn't been painful, more of a shock really. All I could think of was proving to my own satisfaction that I was gamer than any of them. Albert had the same attitude towards the gang, he'd face any odds and never run away.

All the more prominent gangs had a certain style or colour by which they could be identified. The gang we fought with mostly were the Calton Tongs. While we wore green polo-neck sweaters and bottle-green suits as our colours, they wore black. The Maryhill Fleet were the most flamboyant of the gangs, with their full-length suede coats and red polo-neck sweaters. They had fleets of scooters displaying an array of side mirrors but very rarely stood their ground in a fight.

The Tongs were different; they would go ahead. After a battle with them one night in George Square I was done for breach of the peace and carrying an offensive weapon, a meat cleaver. This was my first appearance in court, and I was terrified. Then I saw Albert and the Bear sitting in the public gallery, so I swaggered all the way to the dock, threw my leather coat over the rail, and grinned throughout the remand notice. The judge continued my bail but asked for two weeks' Borstal reports before sentencing me, so I walked out the court laughing. He couldn't give me Borstal then because I was only fifteen years old. You had to be sixteen before they could give you Borstal – and anyway there was no danger of that happening, surely?

A few days later, in a café, I got into a fight with Wee Joe. He was trying to prove that he was more game than everyone else, telling the birds stories about himself. We got into an argument about it. He pinned my hand to the table with a blade during the fight: I smashed a bottle over his head just before the fight was broken up by the others.

Before this row developed into something more serious I found myself back at court for sentencing on the breach and offensive weapon charges. I'd just turned sixteen two days before the court appearance, but I hadn't thought for a moment that I'd get Borstal, which could mean anything from a year to two years locked up in Polmont Borstal Institution.

My granny was the only one in court for me. There were no pals to egg me on, just me and my granny – and that was one of the last times I saw her alive. Sherriff Middleton looked down his nose at her as she tried to appeal to him not to send me away. My legs were trembling but I shouted at him, 'Fuck you, ya fuckin' auld bastard!'

I was held in Barlinnie's Borstal wing for two weeks before being transferred to Friarton Detention Centre. At Barlinnie's reception area I was put into a tiny room the size of a cupboard, which they call the Dog Box, and told to strip off all my clothes. Jesus, was this where I was to be kept for two years? I read all the names scratched on the walls and then the door swung back and a warder in a white medical coat told me to go and see the doctor.

'Name? Religion? Ever had crabs? Okay, bend over.'

I felt like a slave on auction with this bastard poking and prodding, but I kept my face expressionless, so already I was winning. I was given bedding that looked as if it had survived the First World War, and shown to my cell. It was a new and dismal world; I buried my head under the dirty blankets to escape it, but I couldn't sleep that night. And so the nightmare began.

● I lay in the cell for several weeks and then was told to inform my relatives that I was being transferred to Friarton to begin my 'training'. Barlinnie was near my home, and somehow that gave me comfort, but Friarton was in the middle of nowhere, surrounded by barbed wire. It seemed the most isolated place on earth, and for good reason. The door of the Transit van was opened and I was dragged by the hair into the reception area. This time I could conceal my embarrassment when I was stripped in front of everyone, and I could conceal my fear.

It was the most brutal regime. If you didn't salute every warder on sight they beat the shit out of you. I buckled under but swore that I'd pay them back. Solitary was no better: you stood to attention behind a Bible in the middle of the cell all day.

One day a warder came to take me to the visiting area. By

Christ, did I have a few things to tell any visitor! The warder warned me that he'd be within earshot and listening to every word – all for my own good, he said sarcastically. In I went, and there sat my dear old granny. I went up to give her a cuddle but the warder shouted, 'Get your arms folded or the visit's over!' Rather than upset my maw, I just smiled and said that everything was okay and that I'd be home soon. With the daily PT I'd become really fit and looked fine; I concentrated on how I was going to get a job again and stay out of trouble when I got out. At the time I really meant it but, like everything else, it was only a dream.

After another month I was among those transferred to Polmont. The routine was basically the same, but from there you could earn your ticket and get out early or, as they phrased it, 'become a better citizen'. It was back to school again, only at a higher level. To my surprise, I settled in quickly: new faces, same machine. For nine months I played their game and kept my nose clean. One day I was playing darts when the house-master of our hall called me into his office.

'Take a seat, Collins. I have to inform you that your grandmother has died.'

I couldn't believe my ears. Auld Cathie? It was impossible! She was my maw, for Christ's sake. I didn't know what to do or say. Images flashed through my mind of her taking us to the pictures, and letting Alex and me hold on to her arms in a kind of sleepwalk all the way home ... That night in my cell I wanted to wipe everything out of sight, but I felt that I couldn't allow the bastards see me break down. This was a new kind of control for me. When the cell door opened my face was a mask: I told the screw to fuck off, and for a few days they left me to myself.

My father was at the funeral, with a prison escort. By 1968 he was in prison again, on another conviction – assault of some kind. This time I was the one who was handcuffed to two screws. Now I was the one staring coldly, looking silently ahead, not permitted a word to my family and kept far from the grave. My father was accompanied by a single copper. His hands were free. I saw him telling someone a joke and laughing. Now I was the hard man.

●   When at last it was time for me to go home, I realized that I didn't have a home to go to. Cathie had gone to live with her boyfriend, the others were married with homes of their own, and Alex had gone to live with Jack. I hoped that Charlie would meet me off the bus. He was always a good laugh and I felt desperately in need of cheering up. There was no elation at being out. I just wanted to forget Borstal and be with my family again. No one was there. I hung around for an hour, then decided to catch a bus for Royston. When I arrived at my old stop, who should be there but Joe the Bear?

After the hugging had stopped, we looked at each other for a few moments and then Joe shouted at the top of his voice, 'Shamrock, ya fuckin' bass!' and that was me home at last. We went off to find Albert and had a welcome-home party at Wee Joe's.

The next day I managed to find Jack's house, and we sat around all day talking and telling jokes. The doorbell went, and in came my mother. I hadn't seen her in a long, long time. I wanted to touch her, but that stuff was for mammie's boys, so I just sat beside her and listened as she talked. She had a house of her own and asked me to live with her, her new partner and their wee boy. I went. I got a job in a factory, loading crates of beer, and for a month everything was all right. Then I began to get restless, so I asked my ma to help me find somewhere else to live. I felt like an outsider in their house. She hesitated but did find me a flat in the Calton area, Tong territory.

One day I was late for work, and the guy in charge kept going on at me about being a ned: 'Think yer a flyman, don't ye?' I'd never spoken to him before. Eventually I said, 'Go an' fuck yourself,' and went to get my jacket. He wanted an apology, but there was no way I would give one, so we faced each other like cowboys in *High Noon*. It's comical now, but at the time all I could see was a little creep throwing his authority about, and all those beatings in the Borstals flashed through my mind. All those beatings from screwed-up little bastards like this nonentity, but this time there was only one of them. I burst out laughing and kicked the shit out of him. Afterwards I felt lousy about it, but he only had himself to blame.

I had to keep the flat going, so for a while I went out with Albert, breaking into shops at night and doing a bit of shoplifting. The money was good, but I did it because I enjoyed the excitement. I became good friends with a guy who'd also been at our school, Peter Blackburn, and he was game for anything. We screwed the shops most of the week and hit the town at the weekends, drinking and fighting with anyone who so much as looked at us. Peter was a tall, good-looking guy, and birds flocked round him; in order to get one for myself, I had to make my name in the Shamrock battles.

Soon I was caught shoplifting, and given six months in the Young Offenders' unit at Barlinnie. The guys there were aged from sixteen to twenty-one (when they became part of the adult population), and in the 1960s most of them were gang members plus a few burglars and thieves.

There was a pecking order in the dining hall, with the Tongs at the top table, then the Shamrock, the Cumbie, the Fleet from Maryhill, Bridgeton Spurs, and then assorted gangs, with the shoplifters last of all. Every night when you were brought back from the dining hall, you would stand outside your cell – if you were serving over eighteen months you were on the top floor and had a single cell; otherwise cells were shared between two or three men – and the screws would be milling about. They all had nicknames. One, who I'll call 'Mugsie', who had a face like a shoebox, a big blue face, and who was very aggressive. He wore the peaked cap and had the first platform shoes I'd ever seen to give him height. There was Chewing-gum Charlie, a vicious bastard. The Principal Officer was always scudding guys. The Senior Officer was a robust little guy with a wee military moustache; he'd probably spent most of his life in the army. He was always blustering and growling at people, and he'd stand with hair-clippers at the ready, calling out as men walked past. We had long hair and long sideburns then, and he'd beckon you over and just clip them off: nothing below the ear, military-style. Thruppeny Hat was very civil and sharp; he could communicate. But the rest of them were extremely aggressive and formed their own huge gang.

Not a day passed without the BU squad giving someone a beating. They got their name from the way they called you out when everyone was locked in his cell after tea. They'd shout out the numbers of cells: 'Forty-five! Thirty-two! Twenty-one! You're to be Brought Up before the Governor, so take your shoes off and go downstairs!'

Everyone knew this meant a Beating Up in the cell which had been converted into an office with a highly polished floor. It would be jam-packed with screws, and two on the door would call out, 'Name and number to the Governor!' and run you into the cell. You'd slide on the floor, and the screws would begin to batter you senseless while the Governor sat there.

When I was taken in they said, 'Ye're the Shamrock, are ye? Well, we run this place, and don't ye ever forget that.'

I remember one occasion, when there was a heat wave, I stripped to the waist in the shed. A screw came over. 'Right, cunt, get the shirt on and get on with your work.'

'Go an' fuck yerself,' I said, 'ya scummy bastard.'

To my amazement, he backed away. I felt like a real hero and the others treated me as one, but that night after tea I got the call. The next thing I knew I was on the floor with about six screws on top of me and a terrible pain in my testicles – no wonder, as one of them was trying to wrench them off. That was the first of many BUs; the punishment cells seemed like a home away from home, but at least I could do my time in peace there.

They chose the men they saw as the 'tickets' – the hard men in the gangs. It was always the same group who were in and out of prison, a hard core of about fifteen. I became very friendly with Ronnie Neeson from the Cumbie (he's now serving a life sentence; he's been on solitary confinement for six years) – the gangs never fought inside the prison. There was a nucleus who were becoming criminals. You could see that they were going to spend the rest of their lives in and out of institutions. Their only experience of prison officers had been aggression and abuse. When they turned twenty-one, the same group began to meet in the adult prisons. The adult system seemed a bit of a joke to us. We'd see the cons who'd come down from Peterhead for annual visits, and thought they must be hard cases because of the rumours about how tough it was up there. They'd be swaggering around, weather-beaten and suntanned, chewing gum. We thought the screws would be terrified of them, but these were the clowns, the mugs of the jail, and behind the scenes, embarrassingly, they sucked up to the screws: 'Aye, boss!' 'Right, boss!' 'Thanks, boss!'

I assaulted one or two of the staff in the Young Offenders, which was unheard of. Ronnie Neeson was retaliating, too, battering screws all the time. I saw how game Ronnie was. The screws stood round in bunches in the dining hall and intimidated everyone. It was Ronnie who broke the ice. He spilt some soup while carrying his tray and deliberately slid on it, finally emptying his tray all over one of the screws. He said he was sorry. 'We'll fuckin see ye the night,' was the reply. If they'd beaten him up there, in public, the whole place might have erupted, whereas when it happened in the office we each turned a blind eye.

'If they touch me the night, Ah'm goin' to break one of their jaws,' said Ronnie to me.

That night I saw him take his socks off at the cell door, and when the screws came to get him he elbowed one, actually broke his nose. Then there was a big scuffle. Everybody was shouting from their cells – Ronnie was well liked in there. About four days later one of the screws – just a daft wee boy, really, whose father worked in the prison – swaggered up to me on the landing and shoved me.

'Whit the fuck are you on?' I said, and threw him back.

He stammered and started shouting, and as he tried to grab me again I head-butted him. That was me committed to it. I got twenty-eight days in the punishment cells. Ronnie was next door to me and shouted through to find out what had happened.

'I battered a screw,' I shouted back, 'an' they battered me tae fuck.'

So, without even realizing it, we'd begun to develop reputations.

● I don't think the Young Offenders is as obviously brutal now but, looking back on it, I can see why the screws formed a gang. It was intimidation, to prevent anything getting out of hand. The effect was to brutalize us, so that when we went into the main prison, where this kind of thing rarely happened, the others would say to us, 'Ye'd better calm down or they'll batter ye.' But our experience told us that they'd batter us anyway, so we became fearless, in a sense, or at least acclimatized to brutality. The older generation couldn't believe it, but as mine moved on to Peterhead, that's when the carry-on started, the rioting and hostages. The authorities had no idea how to deal with it. Their brutality had backfired on them.

● I found myself in and out of prison regularly over the next ten years, mostly for petty crimes, but the months inside accumulated fast and furious, so that there came a point where I was spending more time inside than outside.

I was sitting in the George Hotel getting drunk one night, when I just decided I'd had enough and wanted to hit the big time: I'd rob a bank. I was almost nineteen years old and still running about like a bampot. Lots of my jail pals had got into bank robberies and jumping shop counters for fast money, serious money: I'd jumped a few counters but had never robbed a bank. The problem had been that I couldn't drive, which was necessary to pull off a bank. Fuck it, I thought. I caught a bus to the Royston Road and got off at the Royal Bank of Scotland. There I was, eyeing the window with a half-brick in my hand – all I needed was the swagbag, a striped jersey and a black mask – when an old face poked out from the flats above and shouted, 'Away ye go, ya silly bugger, before the polis get ye!'

I jumped in fright and shouted something back at her, then walked away, muttering. I looked up as I was passing a fruit shop, and suddenly all I wanted was one of those big red apples, so I levered off the window-guard and heaved in the brick. It was like Aladdin's cave. I sat there for about half an hour, then some people passed and asked me to throw some fruit out. So I did – apples, bananas, oranges, the street was covered with them. Then a big, deep voice said, 'Bring out some sweeties,' and there I was, straight into a copper's arms. I kept my head down in embarrassment from the minute I was arrested until I hit the Dog Box in Barlinnie.

This was a short sentence, but in the course of it something changed. I'd never written to my mother or anyone else when I was in jail because I felt they had their own lives to lead. I was always being told that my da was a real hard case. Now as I lay in my cell I thought about him and how he felt about my mother taking up with another man, and it hurt me deep down. What kind of a bitch was my ma to do that, with my da lying in a cell for ten years? That night I cried myself to sleep, and swore to make my da proud of me, no matter who was hurt or what it cost me. The next morning I woke up determined that I'd make my name, a name my da would hear about. A kind of monster developed in me from that point.

CHAPTER FIVE

———————————●———————————

ALBERT, THE BEAR and Wee Joe were my family now,
my brothers. When they met me from prison, the Bear
recounted the gang's exploits, described the slashings in
detail. Wee Joe handed me an open razor – a pearl-handled
barber's razor – for slashing people. It was good to be out.

My father had taken great pride in my being in one of the
city's most prominent gangs: his boy, a leader of the Shamrock.
He'd introduce me as such to his friends, describing violent gang
incidents.

I recall him one day emerging from a car with three other
men, all immaculately dressed in long, black cashmere coats and
expensive suits, all – with one exception, Collie Beattie – bearing
facial scars, scars worn with pride. Albert and I revelled in their
acknowledgement. This was 'recognition'. We were being hon-
oured by men feared throughout the criminal world. Glasgow
hard men, proving that we were also hard, that we were
different, that we were somebodies.

Collie Beattie was the most respected man in the city. He
never used weapons and spoke like a gentleman, but when he
got going he was something else – he went berserk, frightening.

Collie's tall and handsome, with jet-black hair. He never

touches drugs. His reputation is such that if somebody wants looking after, he's capable of doing it verbally. His prowess as a fighter is legendary throughout the criminal world. He's never been beaten in a fight, and he's fought hard men from different areas of Glasgow and from other parts of Scotland. One guy from the hills came to fight him in a square-go – a big guy weighing sixteen or seventeen stone – and was battered absolutely senseless by the side of a canal.

My da took me to his house after the murder. Collie was a fixer, he could sort out things. He'd have sorted things on the night of the murder if it hadn't all gone so wrong. I could have gone to him for help myself but you don't go running to other people when you're in trouble, you deal with it yourself or you're just a prick.

'What we'll do,' he said, 'is put you into America. I don't think you'll last very long, but that's the best I can do for you, son.'

I would never have been arrested if he'd been in the house that night. The coppers waited until he went out before they burst in. Years ago it had taken twenty-two policemen to get him into a police van. The whole street was out. The police had broken arms, broken jaws and broken noses. That's the only time he's ever been arrested. He is left alone – the police, too, respect him. I said to them in the car that night, 'Fuckin' arseholes! You'd never have come near the door if the Big Yin had been in the house.'

They just laughed and said, 'Fuckin' right!'

● I loved this lifestyle. I enjoyed the women. I loved walking into nightclubs or hotel lounges and feeling the women look at me, wanting me because I was dangerous. Many did want me for just that reason, and it reinforced my drive for prominence in the gang. Albert and I dressed in style. We could well afford tailor-made suits, expensive coats and shoes. We could have had formal eight-to-five jobs, but why work when you could just take things? This was the world we grew up in, a world where violence flourished and was never questioned, where violent men were respected and esteemed.

Albert and I didn't drink any more. We both trained, to be fast in a fight – especially Albert, who was fanatical about being fit, a natural athlete. I trained in order to feel good and look good. Well dressed, with lots of cash, extremely fit, we knew that we were feared. Doormen all over the city centre knew who we were; doormen and bar staff, even in the trendiest places, knew the consequences of ever crossing the Shamrock mob.

This fear and the glamour were strong motivations for many of the gang, and undeniably for me. But there was more than mere vanity binding us: we'd grown up together. The Bear and Wee Joe were hopeless shoplifters; they didn't bother about training, they both liked to drink. Albert and I were the opposite: we were excellent thieves and hated drinking. Our bond was the Shamrock: we were the Shamrock and the rest were, in a sense, outsiders. What had begun as boys hanging out together had developed into a violent gang who used weapons. There seems an inevitability about it all, a deadly certainty about its final destination.

Fear also played its part among us. I have never taken part in a fight without the dread of being slashed or stabbed, of dying or being sent to prison. My legs used to shake, my stomach churned, my bowels were about to give way. I sweated profusely. No matter whom I faced I feared that I might come off second-best, take a second prize. The fear of losing face, the fear that Albert might see my deep alarm, was even stronger – this fear of being exposed as a coward was what drove me. The physical actuality of the violence was a relief: I felt the pleasure of its release, a pure sensation.

I have no doubt that the others experienced fear. Once Albert, Wee Joe and his sister were waiting for the Bear in a hotel lounge. When he eventually arrived, he was raging: some guy in a bar had made a fool of him. The Right Half bar belonged to Arthur Thomson, a genuine gangster who had been involved in murders; the guy in question worked for him and had just finished a ten-year prison sentence. The Bear wanted him done: fuck Thomson. Wee Joe's sister lured the guy outside under some pretext, and we battered him unconscious in the doorway. A special police squad just happened to pass by: when their van screeched to a halt we scattered, but one by one we were caught and battered in the van. The Bear was picked up last and suffered the least on the journey to the police station; Albert had been thrown on top of me and had taken the brunt of the beating. The Bear, however, had shit himself with fear, and the awful smell filled the van; police were holding their noses. Albert and I couldn't stop laughing as the Bear changed his underwear in the cell and threatened us not to tell anyone. Obviously we wouldn't have, and the Bear played it down the next day when we were released. The guy we had battered didn't press charges, so we were bruised but free to go.

Fear is something you admit to no one: few people admit it to themselves. The fear is there, though; it's always there, no matter who you think you are.

CHAPTER SIX

●

THE GANG SCENE changed in the 1960s, with the introduction of drugs. It seemed to happen overnight, but that was because I'd been in Borstal, out of the way. When Albert met me, he said, 'Wait till you see this mob the night.'

We were going to meet everyone at the One Four Lounge. People who had been pretty violent in the gang had suddenly become hippies: long hair, speaking like Americans: 'Yeah, man, everything's cool.' I didn't know what was going on. I had an open razor on me, cropped hair, a suit: they had beads and caftans. They were all into hash, Albert said, and acid. There were massive amounts of LSD around. Hash cost £7 for a quarter ounce, £14 for a half and £28 for an ounce. Most of the drugs were coming from Manchester, London and Liverpool.

I'd read about LSD but I'd never tried it. Before I'd gone to Borstal I'd tried hash and pep pills, blues and bombers. Johnny Gemmell had taken me to a flat in the West End where a Jamaican guy had been blowing on a pipe and had given me a few draws. At first I didn't feel anything, then I turned chalk-white and began talking a lot of nonsense; eventually I couldn't stop giggling. Afterwards I was reluctant to take drugs because of the effect that hash had on me. I was scared that I might get chibbed while I was on the stuff. I'd read about LSD – people seeing elephants and thinking they could fly – and I didn't like the sound of that at all.

Sauchiehall Street had been transformed: lots of nightclubs, people selling dope, hippie bands. When I was sent to Borstal they'd been listening to Motown; now it was all heavy progressive stuff. Johnny Gemmell knew that Albert and I enjoyed violence, and wanted to recruit us to move in on the drug scene. At this time the Drug Squad was forming, and we regarded them as a joke. The Untouchables were more familiar to us, plain-clothes police who patrolled the city centre in a blue van. They had their fingers on the button: they knew who to look for whenever there was a slashing or a stabbing; they put me in Borstal. If they pulled you and you didn't have a knife on you, you laughed at them, but if they caught you with as much as a penknife, then they went overboard to get you.

● Albert's been telling me things have changed – but this? I just can't believe what's happening. The bouncers nod, but I recognize hardly anyone. Nobody carries blades. Nobody wants trouble. Someone's talking to me from behind a bush of hair; he looks like a holy picture. Fuck, it's Peter Blackburn! I can't take this in: Peter's one of the boys. What's he doing like this?

The music is almost deafening. Albert is looking on, seemingly uninterested. He's still immaculate, hair cropped to the skull, cold black eyes watching every move. He's leaving to meet a bird. Peter's telling me about acid parties. Acid parties? He's tossing his hair to the music and playing an invisible guitar. The whole place is jumping: long hair and invisible guitars.

'Here, Collie, swallow these man. It's some heavy speed, man.'

I like pep pills, bombers mostly. These tablets are tiny, wrapped in Cellophane. I swallow them and finish my drink. I'm going to Possilpark to see my Aunty Mary, hoping that her prick of a husband isn't there.

What was that? I'm walking up Sauchiehall Street and a wall's painted surface just made a hissing sound, or was it a car passing? What made that noise? It went right past my ear. There's a taxi, I'll take it.

'Possilpark, driver.'

What's he staring at? Is he staring at me in his mirror?

'Here, driver, whit's aw the starin' about?'

He's not even listening.

'Here, are you fuckin' deaf?'

He doesn't know what I'm talking about.

'Ye didnae say anythin', son.'

He's trying to be clever now.

'Well, jist stop the starin', okay?'

'Aye, sure, son, whatever you say.'

He heard me that time, the fucking bampot. Why aren't we moving? What – we're here?

'Aye, son. We've bin here fur aboot ten minutes. Are ye payin' the fare then?'

My Aunty Mary's house is like Santa's grotto. There are ornaments everywhere, millions of them, in brass, glass, plastic, china. There's a photograph of me on the wall: a wee fat face in a cowboy hat. My Uncle George doesn't fit in, sitting there in his string vest, his fat belly squeezing through the holes. I hate him; he used to lock me in a dark room with a big dog. He's a bully, but I battered him. George tells lies to sound tough. He's doing it now, telling me lies; I can actually see them pouring out of him. That scar on his face is a cracker: I wonder who done him – my da?

Jesus Christ! The wallpaper is moving, the patterns are bending. That wee globe just exploded into colours! Jesus, I can't stop laughing, my whole body is shaking. Hell, George is changing shape! His jaws are getting bigger and slavering like an animal's, he's turning into a grotesque ogre. The whole room is changing, moving, becoming merely colours. My head is exploding. There's music coming from inside my brain, violins are playing, tubas bursting – millions of noises. What's George doing? He's planning to kill me. I can hear his mind. He hasn't a face, the features are breaking up, colours flying past his ears. Don't look at him. Fuck, I can't move. I don't know how to lift my arm, nothing will move. But nothing is still – God, these feelings, overwhelming feelings, of absolute joy. These tears, what are they? There are no words where I am, no description, only motion, everything in motion, nothing is still. The image looking at me is beautiful: is it a painting? There is a thing behind me, it's laughing in my ear ... Something's frightening me. The hall is dark, there are things watching, I can see them moving, shadows touching me. The kitchen: look at all these things sparkling – shining, wonderful objects. I fill my pockets with knives, forks, spoons, anything that glitters; the kitchen is so bright, everything is a mass of colour, wonderful, vibrant, living colour. There is stuff spewing out of my mouth; bits of stomach falling and splattering against a silver bowl. The sink is half-filled with vomit, things that look like tiny faceless babies, like coils of intestines, squelching green membranes, heaving and swirling down the hole. I wonder what's down there – is it my stomach? Put them back in. That's it, push it back down; eat more and everything will be okay.

There are moaning noises, something's groaning somewhere. This place is black, it's like a blanket of thick blackness. The moaning is louder, moving, thrashing around. Every part of my body is trembling: what's that noise? The sudden flash of light is blinding: George and Mary naked, their sweating, bloated bodies one on top of the other, trembling, fatty flesh like waves of shimmering meat. They're having sex, fucking. A shudder ripples through my body, a sexual wave of sheer ecstasy. George is pulling me out of the room: 'For fuck's sake, whit are you on?' He's locking me somewhere – in the toilet. There are plants everywhere, looking at me, dancing for me. There are no barriers, no divisions between us. The dirt is moving, everything is moving; there is no me, only a single motion. My face in a mirror: flowing skin, changing endlessly, another face, racing flashes of colour; black eyes, pupils completely dilated, flickering film, a river of colour. Shudders ripple through my whole body, my heart speeding with excitement, my penis hard and erect, straining to feel a caress. I can't stand on my shaking legs. The floor is a mass of small insects bustling around; I lie with them, naked, hearing every hurried noise, watching every movement, masturbating. Shocks rush through my body, sexual thrills over and over, exploding into a mass of colour. Colour explodes from my head, receding as my orgasm subsides; semen over my stomach and chest, a salty taste in my mouth. My eyes roll, staring into my skull; everything is on fire. I can only lie there, staring, totally incapable of functioning.

Sixteen hours have passed. I'm still in the toilet. Mary's at the door. 'Are ye okay, son?' Aunty Mary: thank fuck. I come out, totally bewildered. Normality is returning but I can't look at anyone. I'm put in a taxi to the Garngad, to Peter's house. What the fuck did he give me? I somehow don't feel the same person.

Peter is in hysterics. He'd given me two tabs of black microdot and blown my brains apart. He could have told me what to expect. I've been insane for sixteen hours, locked in my own nightmare ... and yet I recall those moments of seeing without divisions, without barriers – moments of absolute beauty.

● I find myself gradually seeing more of Peter. He introduces me to a different world: the hippy bars, the acid parties and the women – the women are into free love. My hair's beginning to grow longer, I'm dressing less formally, I'm taking drugs fairly regularly – acid and hash – but in controlled situations, with pals. I'm attracted to the freedom of the lifestyle, and to the women, but I'm still close to Albert. He's still a brother.

Peter's terrified of Albert, and I don't blame him. Albert's a frightening figure – the cropped hair and black eyes, the coldness, the fanatical fitness, everything geared for violence. Albert scares me, too, but I've nothing to fear. We've grown up together, thieving, fighting, never questioning each other; we're never apart. Peter freaks out whenever he's around, but I suspect it's the acid; he's into it in a big way, tripping every couple of days, wandering round graveyards, out of his skull.

With Albert there's power: the two of us together are a bad combination, people fear us. We do everything together: if Albert decides he wants to slash someone, I'm right behind him, and vice versa. When we enter a nightclub we can feel the fear and we play on that. Albert hates drugs and drinks, especially the drugs. He hates that whole world. The long-hairs are alien to him: 'They all look like fuckin' birds.' He's a naturally quiet guy, but people pick up vibes from him, and it freaks them out.

Peter's having an influence on me. I'm going to more and more parties with him, becoming overwhelmed by the whole scene. People are injecting drugs now, jagging morphine, speed, heroin, almost anything. The LSD is knocking me off my head; I'm beginning to experience paranoia and deep fears – fears of being attacked, of being jailed. I'm always waiting for something to happen. The parties are changing; people are trying to play mind-games, fucking round with people's heads. There are no women hanging round, and it's all getting a bit weird.

The occult is creeping into the scene: people are reading books like *The Devil Rides Out* and want to have black masses. The light-hearted stuff has become boring: they want something more serious, more sophisticated.

One night there are four of us in a guy's flat, on strong acid. He is supposed to be able to handle acid, and he decides to play the game with me, saying he wants to have a black mass.

'Go ahead,' I say. 'Does the Devil appear here on a Saturday night because you're on a trip?'

He says they need a sacrifice, and I say I'll get one. He has a cat. I go into the kitchenette and get hold of the cat by the neck – it's clawing me to bits. I pick up a tin-opener, and just press it into the cat, and end up killing it. I think I know what I am doing but it isn't violent, it's simply curiosity.

I've been out there for about an hour, and meanwhile some

girls have come up to the flat and they've all drifted into a totally different state, up in the clouds again. I pull the door open and say, 'I've got that sacrifice.' That freaks them right out. The guy that owns the flat jumps straight out the window and bolts.

Albert pulls me out of it. 'C'mon, Collie, let's head down to Manchester.'

● On the very day we arrive, we meet a guy selling black bombers – pep pills. He wants £1 a head, which is a bit expensive.

'How many have ye got, pal?'

'Er, about five 'undred, mate.'

'Okay, let's do the deal somewhere quiet. There's a toilet.'

The razor at his throat convinces him to part with the pills without any fuss. Albert's laughing, but I know he'll slash the guy if he makes one wrong move. We leave him there with a warning not to try anything stupid when we get outside. Albert's still smiling. 'Nae hard feelings, pal.'

I keep some of the pills and sell the remainder; they're popular with women dieting to lose weight fast, and great for nightclubbing into the late hours.

Albert knows some black guys in Moss-Side. He's done time with them: 'Let's go and see them. They're good guys, Collie.' Reggae, hash and women. I'm having a ball. The nightclubs are lively, we're being looked after, everyone's friendly towards us, everything's really cool. Albert's liked by these people, they respect us, it's mutual. I find the black women amazing – I dance all night with one, and end up fucking her in bed.

Manchester's great. We're shoplifting during the day and clubbing at night. Our flat is sparse – stolen suits line the walls, a stereo lifted from a shop display and loads of other stolen gear. We take orders in the morning and deliver the goods that day to the punters. We're providing a service – cash on delivery, it's good business, everyone's happy.

The Moss-Side clubs are good but we like to move around, try different places. Our Scottish accents attract women somehow, they find it amusing. Men find themselves drawn to it too, but for different reasons: 'You two gits down from Scotland?'

Albert and I are surrounded by bouncers in a nightclub. They're pushing for trouble – we aren't carrying any weapons. 'You cunts is out of order. What you think you're on, mate? Think this is fuckin' Scotland? What?'

We're lifted bodily, taken down a corridor and battered. I'm held down and systematically pounded. My face looks like a bruised football: my nose is fractured, my eyes are blackened. Albert's no better – his mouth's cut open inside, it's pretty bad. We don't know what happened, they just moved in on us – anyway we're not interested.

We're back two days later, speeding and tooled up with steak knives. We're waiting in a car by the kerb when we see three of them as they emerge from the nightclub. Albert's first out of the car. 'Right, Collie, c'mon. Let's do these fuckin' pricks!'

Albert strikes the first guy over the head twice with the steak knife. Blood spurts on to the wall. What the fuck . . . ? They don't know what's hit them. I've slashed one in the face; he's burst wide open. I'm on another guy's back, hitting him over the head with the blade. I heard the noises, metal on skull, clunk! clunk! Two are on their knees, bleeding onto the pavement. Albert goes for one again, opening up another cut.

'Right, c'mon, let's get to fuck.'

I kick one in the face. English fuckin' bampots!

I look back from the car. They're still on the ground; one is staggering to his feet. The fight has lasted no more than a few seconds.

'We done the bastards, Albert. We fuckin' done the three pricks!'

Albert doesn't say much, but we're both high and laughing.

'Did ye see that cunt's face? They weren't expecting that, eh? The fuckin' bampots!'

We decide that staying on would be too risky and return to Glasgow.

● Albert stays at his ma's and I spend a few days with my old man. He's drinking heavily, but I don't mind. He talks about the jail, and the laughs he had, but never about the painful part. Betty Norrie? He sings about her over and over – something about passing strangers. I feel tears welling up. How could she have abandoned him? Why couldn't she have waited for him? We could have been a family . . .

Peter's still doing drugs, he takes me to a party and as soon as the front door opens a guy asks, 'Are ye trippin', man?'

When I say, 'No,' he sticks a tab of acid in my mouth. I manoeuvre it under my tongue, intending to spit it out, but the stuff melts.

Once these parties began in a nice, relaxed way with music like the Moody Blues. Now people are bored with all that. They want something more sophisticated to test their acid perceptions on – and they've no idea of the dangers.

I'm beginning to feed on fear – other people's fears. I can pick up on them and get an intensified sense of power. I'm sitting with three guys, all complete strangers. Peter's sitting on a chair opposite me, staring; the paranoia is ripping out of him. Someone is talking, his face totally distorted, whispering to his friends. It seems conspiratorial.

'Collie, sit o'er here wi' me,' Peter says urgently.

A thousand miles lie between us: a coffee table. I have to pass the strangers on the way. They look like a three-headed monster, squirming around, six rolling eyes, gaping mouths slavering.

'Collie, sit o'er here wi' me.'

I pass them, and pull out a bayonet from under my coat. 'Here. Dae ye's want a real fuckin' party?'

One guy vomits all over the place. Then, 'Aw, man, please! Naw, man, nae violence.'

His two pals take the horrors.

I enjoy every minute.

Peter freaks out. 'Collie! The Devil's inside ye. Look at yer eyes, look at yer eyes, man. It's Satan, man!'

Albert's killing himself laughing when he hears. The Devil? That big yin's a fuckin' headcase.

Albert's more interested in making money. We're pushing things, marching into clothes shops and just taking what we want. We discover guys who'd been in other gangs now working in city-centre tailors'; suits are just there for the taking through threats. We're doing things all over the city, and then we meet Big Tam, an ex-copper now working as a chargehand in the George Hotel. He can't understand why we waste so much energy on violence without making any real profits. 'Why don't you hit the brewery pubs?' he suggests. 'They'll lose their licences if they have repeated incidents. You could fire into them for protection.'

We start at the Lunar Seven and within weeks we're working our way right along Sauchiehall Street every Friday night, collecting money from pubs and bands and hash from dealers. Albert is delighted with just going into pubs and intimidating people. We're getting around £2,000–£2,500 a week between us, and he doesn't drink or smoke. He's always getting measured for suits, buying PT gear. He enjoys having money. Both of us grew up poor, so he likes to have lots of money in his pocket.

The Bear has been involved with some bird, hardly seeing any of the boys, but he's back on the scene again and declares himself in. The Trianon Lounge hosts a band at weekends, and Albert and I have already told the band members that they're paying us a tenner each to play – there are seven members. The Bear decides to collect the money. Albert and I can't be bothered going all the way back down Sauchiehall Street; we'll catch him later. The Trianon's busy, and the band's good. The Bear pulls the singer.

'Ye got the money, pal?'

'Whit money?'

'The fuckin' protection money.' 'Ah'm Joe Bear.'

'Are ye? Right, yer done! I'm Detective Sergeant . . .'

Albert and I can't stop laughing when we hear what's happened. The band had reported us to the coppers, and he walks straight into it. Ah'm Joe the Bear. Aye, and we're Strathclyde Police.

At Glasgow High Court the Bear is sentenced to four years – the only extortionist never to collect his money.

● My experience is different. For example: a publican approached me and asked me to slash someone who is giving him trouble; he'll pay a hundred quid. I slashed the man and collected the money. The next week I returned for another hundred. The publican was surprised to see me and refused to pay. I returned the following week and this time demanded two hundred – one hundred for this week, one hundred for the week before. Again he refused to pay, but I could tell he was frightened. And with good reason.

In this new Glasgow, my success rested on my reputation for limitless violence. I was both menace and protector, and I couldn't be one effectively without being the other. When the publican refused to make the payment, he knew that he'd eventually have trouble. He made a further mistake. Just as he'd hired me to slash a man who had been a problem, so he now asked his bouncer to slash me – for a hundred quid. But I heard about that from a friend.

The bouncer didn't have to look for me. I presented myself at the pub the same evening. He was at the door.

'Are ye lookin' for me?' I asked. I stepped right up to him, my face inches from his, an open razor in the palm of my hand.

'Why, Collie,' he said, surprised but very friendly. 'How're ye doin'?'

I reached up behind him, grabbed him by the hair, jerked his head back and slashed him straight along the right jaw line, the blood spurting suddenly onto my face and hair and shirt, a steady stream. He buckled, and I pulled back harder on his hair.

'Naw, mate,' he said, 'I'm not looking for you. There's been some mistake.'

'Yer right there's been some mistake,' I said. 'Tell yer fuckin' gaffer he owes me money.' And then I slashed him across the other side of his jaw line.

I had known, from the moment I'd heard the news that morning, what I was going to have to do that evening. The entire operation was carried out mechanically: no reflection, no regrets. It was business. But then, later that night, when I was at home smoking a joint, relaxing, I saw his face, the way the skin was stretched as I pulled at his hair, the expression of fear in his eyes. It made me sick.

Lately I've realized that I was always revolted by violence when the recipient collapsed in on himself, like that bouncer – a sherracking would have been enough. It was different when a guy was ready and wanted to challenge me. Then I felt victorious when I beat him, and no remorse. I've got to equate that with the reaction in war: after a battle, a man doesn't suddenly turn round and say, 'Oh, I took a liberty there.' He feels that same sense of victory I felt when someone was tooled up to meet me and I made a worse mess of him than he made of me.

Most criminal autobiographies lean on black-outs, glossing over the facts. It's amazing how many murderers can't recall actually killing a person. What I'm describing here is the ugliness of gratuitous violence. Is there any other kind?

CHAPTER SEVEN

———————●———————

SOME ODD EVENTS follow, and lead to the most violent period of a violent life. It starts quietly enough, when Albert and Wee Joe decide to take a walk down to the Calton. We aren't carrying any blades, we're just going down to see a couple of guys. Harry Sloan's with us; he's a guy from our area, not involved in anything. The Tongs run this district, but the gangs are breaking up. People are more interested in earning money now.

Rab MacInteer was in approved school with Wee Joe. We meet him at a café and have coffee together. Everything's fine, there's no atmosphere, everyone's cool with each other. When we get up to go, the mood changes; Rab's eyes are darting all over the place. I'm looking at him: there's definitely something wrong. He's expecting something, fidgeting, looking over our shoulders.

'Tongs! Tongs!'

I hear the cry go up just before I feel the blade in my back.

'Tongs! Tongs!'

I'm pushed forward by the blow but steady myself and run. People are scattering everywhere. Harry Sloan dives into a close, followed by two guys waving meat cleavers and bayonets. There's no sign of Albert or Wee Joe.

'Tongs! Tongs!'

They're after me. Blood is running into my shoes; my feet are squelching; the stab wound's burning. I feel dizzy but manage to keep going until it's safe to slow down. Fuck! We've been set up.

Harry Sloan is in intensive care. He's lost two fingers and been slashed all over – legs, body, face. The police want a statement.

'Big Harry's told us everything. He'll be lucky to last the night.'

Albert and I are arrested the following day as I'm signing myself out of hospital. Wee Joe is already at the station when we arrive, drinking tea. The police describe in detail what happened the previous night, but I distort the facts by giving false descriptions of the assailants. By now I know that one was Benny Fisher, the leader of the Tongs. Later that night he was arrested after another incident in Bridgeton.

Wee Joe decides to head down south. Albert decides on Manchester. Harry Sloan's in a real mess, and they don't want to be dragged into a murder trial. Manchester doesn't appeal to me. I tell Albert I'll wait to see what happens and be down in a couple of weeks.

Peter has heard about the trouble and is relieved that Albert is going to Manchester. He is doing drugs with Johnny but they're having difficulty getting hold of the stuff: dealers are scarce because trouble's expected, or perhaps it's some sort of retaliation – everyone stays away. Peter and I are stoned on phycepton tablets, a substitute for heroin. We meet some guys and arrange a party, and on the way down Sauchiehall Street I lose sight of Peter. The city centre is heaving with people, and all of a sudden someone punches me on the jaw, then kicks me as I try to get to my feet. What the fuck's going on? Who are these guys?

Peter finds me and we see the two guys waiting at a bus stop nearby. I wrap a leather belt around my hand; the buckle is like a knuckle-duster. I punch the first guy straight out. His head clatters against a wall, his eye cut wide open. Peter has hold of the other guy; the buckle bursts his mouth and his eye opens next.

'Collie, that's enough man! C'mon before the coppers come, for fuck's sake!'

Too late: two coppers grab me. I'm charged with resisting arrest and two serious assaults. I have a black eye in the morning from the fight. The coppers did the rest – five stitches in my head, par for the course.

● After three months without bail, I'm sentenced to twelve months in Barlinnie. For some reason Sheriff Bell is sympathetic; he seems genuinely concerned about my involvement with drugs. He takes the three months on remand into consideration when sentencing me; in all, I'll serve six months in prison. I have no regrets about the two guys. They poured it on thick in court: two innocent bystanders having a night out . . .

The prison sentence provides a temporary break from drugs – and from criminal activities. I meet an old pal from Borstal, Nada; I can't believe it when he tells me he's serving a life sentence for murder. I'm fascinated but don't dare ask how he feels, nor do I mention my sentence again. Fucking hell – *life*: how does that feel?

● On the day I'm released, I'm to appear as a Crown witness against Benny Fisher in the case of Harry Sloan. Joe has been cited, too, but he has mysteriously gone on the run. Albert has a doctor's line stating that he's suffering from concussion. He just doesn't want anything to do with courts. Benny Fisher's out on bail. We meet outside the court.

'Whit's the score, Collie? Are ye stickin' me in too?'

'Whit dae ye mean? Who's stickin' you in?'

'Look, Wee Joe gave a statement against me, and so did his sister. Sloan's evidence can't do me on its own, but the two of yer statements is corroboration.'

I can't believe what he's saying. Wee Joe's made a statement against him? I recall the tea at the police station, and now he's on the run . . . I feel embarrassed.

'Look, Benny, Sloan's definitely grassing. I know that for a fact. I've told the coppers that I didn't recognize anyone that night. You don't have to worry about me. By the way, it's no finished yet.'

An hour later I'm down in the cells of the High Court, charged with perjury. The coppers verballed me up – I can't fucking believe it. How fucking stupid can you get? The bastards have asked me to go back in the box and to tell the truth this time.

'Fisher might walk, Collins. Believe me, if he does, you can expect about ten years.'

'Whit? You bastards verballed me up! Fuck you an' yer ten years!'

Fisher is found not proven in our case, but gets twelve years for the Bridgeton charge.

● Three months later, at Edinburgh High Court, I'm sentenced to eighteen months in a Young Offenders' institution. After a brief period in Barlinnie, I'm allocated to Pentland Hall in Saughton Prison. I'm relieved that the sentence isn't more severe, but I feel angry. Eighteen months for what – getting myself stabbed? I'm bitter about the whole episode. Albert provides everything I need and writes regularly. My da's proud that I haven't grassed anyone, I haven't let him down. I hate the fucking place and rebel from start to finish; I'm in solitary confinement throughout the sentence, losing all my remission.

● When we're out and about again, Albert wants me to go with him to Manchester. Wee Joe's living in Coventry; Albert doesn't believe he's a grass and nothing will convince him otherwise. Things have changed, we're having to go out grafting again – but that's what we enjoy, isn't it?

Johnny's looking for us. He's setting up arrangements with drug dealers. The Drug Squad have established themselves, terrorizing people everywhere. The modified hippy look is the thing now: flared jeans, platform shoes, feather-cut hairstyles, maybe a bangle. I look like the thug I am, with my cropped hair. Johnny thinks our appearance could be useful. 'Why don't you two kid on ye're the Drug Squad when there's a deal goin' down?'

The Maryland Club has a system to deal with an unexpected visit from the Drug Squad: they flick the stage lights and everyone dumps their dope. When Albert and I appear in suits on the night of a benefit performance after the Ibrox stadium disaster, what happens? Yes, the lights flick on and off. Conveniently enough, Johnny is already there. Albert and I simply walk round the place picking up the abandoned caches: hash, cocaine, sulph, smack, all sorts. Johnny knows the dealers doing cocaine, so he hangs on to that – he's jagging. Albert and I sell our cut.

Sometimes we also arrest Johnny just as he's making a deal. What a coincidence: the Drug Squad! Nobody move! Up against the wall! The client inevitably makes a run for it and manages to get away – minus either cash or dope. Unfortunately, one guy, carrying a thousand tabs of acid, tries to put up a struggle. He freaks out when he sees our razors. Jesus! The D. S. have knives! When I slash him, he freaks out even more. The Drug Squad had a bad name, but I guess this was taking things a bit too far. We had a few months and then they were on to us.

● Albert and I decide to go back to Manchester. We launch ourselves into a shoplifting spree, working from eight in the morning until teatime. We have our old contacts, with even more orders, and everyone's making a profit. Albert's bird has a wee boy. He's delighted to be a father, and absolutely dotes on his son. I'm happy, too; there's lots of money coming in, it couldn't be better.

'Collie, Wee Joe's in trouble,' says Albert. 'He wants us to go through to Coventry.'

Albert doesn't believe anything I've told him, but he's the best mate I have. I can't refuse him. When we arrive in Coventry, we spot velvet suits in a shop window. We've never grafted here.

'Albert, fancy a look tae see whit they suits are like?'

Ten minutes later, we're being chased for our lives. Four store detectives want the suits back and they're running. We reach a canal.

'Albert, honest, Ah cannae run!'

'Right, Collie! C'mon, then, dive in.'

I take him literally and dive head first. Splosh! I hit the bottom of the canal, trapping myself on a spoke embedded in oily mud. I'm flapping like mad but getting nowhere, spluttering and choking, panic-stricken. Albert drags me up by the hair and onto the embankment; we're covered in a black oil slick from head to toe. A detective, to top it all, hits me bang on the back of the head with a half-brick.

'Ya bastard! Two daft fuckin' suits? Ya fuckin bampots, ye's!'

After about two hours of wandering round, we find Wee Joe. I'm in bed for days afterwards, totally knackered with flu. Wee Joe's been having trouble, sure enough, but it was sorted out before we arrived. Could Benny Fisher have been lying, trying to mix it?

● When we get back to Manchester, two guys from Glasgow are waiting at our flat, Jack Cousins and James McCourt. Jack has lots of hash and pills. Albert doesn't stop grafting, and wants me out with him, but I'm mostly too stoned. The truth is that my bottle's crashed – my nerve's gone. I can't shake off almost drowning in the canal. Albert's pissed off but I don't notice until one night at the flat he turns on me with a razor, misses me by inches. What the fuck's happening? We're brothers, aren't we? He's just tried to rip me! I'm shattered.

'Collie, ye'd better have the rent money when I get back tonight. I'm fuckin' warnin' ye.'

I decide to return to Glasgow, and leave him to think things through. I just can't believe this attitude. Has Wee Joe said something to him, trying to mix things too? What the fuck's wrong with him? We've never had this. Jack helps pack my gear.

'Listen, Collie, here's an address for the night. I'll meet ye there later. I'm no stayin' here wi' that fuckin' nutcase – he'll probably do me as well.'

When Jack turns up that evening, he's wearing a jacket that looks like Albert's. Jesus Christ! He's taken everything! Albert will kill him.

'Jack, are ye aff yer fucking head? He'll go fuckin' crazy when he finds out. Ye'd be better tae take it back before he tipples.'

'Collie, he was gonny chib the two of us anyway, so fuck him.'

I'm tempted to go back, but Albert's liable to do me without asking questions. I just don't know where I stand with him, and I don't want to end up with a sore face. Jesus, he'll probably think it was me after the carry-on back at the flat. I don't know how to sort this out; it's almost impossible without trouble.

● Jack and I are stoned for weeks. We find ourselves in Liverpool. I can't steal any more without panicking, not even from supermarkets. And Jack's no better, which narrows our chances. Glasgow seems the only alternative to starving.

'Jack, let's head up the road. I'm fuckin' sick of this. We'd better be prepared for trouble, though. Albert's bound to be lookin' for us.'

CHAPTER EIGHT

———————————●———————————

PETER HASN'T HEARD anything at all. 'Naw, Albert's still in Manchester, Collie.'

He's been put onto a turn, a snatch from a night-safe. 'Collie, this is a cakewalk. There's two birds wi' the takings fae a shop in the toon. All we do is take it, an' they get their cut later. Are ye in?'

We lift two grand and just walk away. After the two birds get their cut, we're out chasing women. I'm getting my confidence back; the future's brighter and we're making money. I get involved with a bird called Eileen. She was married to Johnny Gemmell, but they're divorced now and he's only interested in seeing their daughter, Lynn. Johnny and I drift back into doing rip-offs with a couple of other guys, occasional snatches from night-safes, even some extortion.

Eileen and I get a house in Springburn. One morning when we're lying in bed there's a knock at the door.

'Post, Mr Collins. Recorded delivery.'

I pull on a pair of jeans to go and sign for it, and when I open the door find two detectives standing there.

'Hello, Hughie! Ye're an awful man tae find. We've been lookin' for ye for a couple of assault an' robberies.'

At the Sheriff's Court I'm sentenced to two years. Eileen promises to wait and write every week. Surprisingly, she does. In jail I become friendly with a guy from Edinburgh called Louis Knowles. Louis is doing heroin, mainlining. I'm curious. 'Whit's that like, Louis, mainlining it?'

'It hits ye straight away, Hughie. There's nae hangin' around waitin' for the stone.'

The belt's tight around my arm, but when it's loosened off it's amazing. You get a rush from your toes up – it's like a train coming right over you. There's a gentle tap on the back of your head and *wham!* Instantly stoned. The contents of your stomach come up, but it's not like retching, it's actually quite pleasant. I lie there lost in dreams, nodding off into a gouch; it's absolute pleasure.

Louis is a very gentle guy, an old hippy, bald with a full beard. He's a serious junkie, and it's easy to see why – heroin has a powerful pull. I leave prison with a very serious habit and no understanding of the implications of addiction.

● Eileen's waiting for me at the station. She has a house for us in Balornock. I've behaved in prison – only one hiccup with a daft screw in the surgery. Now I'm out and about again, and it feels good to be free.

Johnny and I are having a drink together in the Blenheim Bar in Sauchiehall Street, and in walk the Blue Angels. They're doing their best to intimidate everyone: dressed in their colours, making mean faces, smelling of oil. One of them recognizes me and says they're looking for a half-pound of hash. Johnny suggests that two of them come with us when we've finished our drinks. We've a pound of hash in the car, parked up a nearby lane. A face with a handlebar moustache speaks – apparently he's the lieutenant.

'Ah'm Papa. Make sure ye've got the dope, man.'

Thor the Viking: leather boots and chains everywhere. I fondle the razor in my pocket.

'Aye, Papa, nae bother. Yer pal gies him the money and I'll gie ye the message, okay?'

Johnny's counting the money at the entrance to the lane. 'Aye, it's all here,' he shouts. 'Five-fifty!'

Papa's asking me what the half-brick in my hand is for.

'This, ya fuckin' clown!'

The brick makes a crunching noise against his nose. I laugh as he falls to his knees, stunned by the blow. I pull his hair back. 'Here's that fuckin' message.'

The razor opens his jaw; blood spatters my jeans. Johnny and I just walk away.

'Fancy a pint up Byres Road?'

● This is the drug scene now: rip-offs, money and violence. Anything goes. Things have soured so rapidly. Am I the cause of the violence?

Some time later I'm in the Maggi Lounge in Sauchiehall Street, selling acid. Peter's with some of the boys in the main bar. The Govan Team are there, too, looking for acid, but they don't want to pay. They think I'm on my own and follow me outside.

'Here, Hector, where's the fuckin' acid?'

I'm being battered with bottles and kicked all over the street. Someone's trying to get into my pockets. Peter and the others spill out. The Goven guys are outnumbered, but there's a brief fight before they scatter. Peter catches one of them. 'Collie! Tan the Prick!'

I slash him from head to toe: *zip, zip, zip!* I do his legs, his hands and his face.

A passing car screeches to a halt and a would-be hero shouts to leave him alone. The razor breaks on the car window as the driver slams the boot down, just barely escaping a sore face. Blood is pouring down my own face from head wounds. The guy on the ground is bleeding, too. He receives the last rites, there on the pavement, from a priest. He does survive, though and some months later, during the murder trial, points me out from the dock. 'Your Honour, I was just out for a quiet night with friends when this man attacked me for no reason.' Yes, an innocent man on a night out . . . Fuck him.

A few weeks later I'm supposed to be meeting Peter. He wants to meet me in Burn's Howf. He pretends he's a foreigner and they fall for it every time, fall for his good looks.

I decide to go over to see my old man first and end up spending a couple of days with him, getting drunk together at wine parties. He wants to try acid. 'Whit's it like, Hughie?'

Jesus, that's all he needs! 'Na, I don't think so, Wullie.'

My da likes me to call him by his first name, especially in women's company. 'Don't call me "da", it makes me feel auld, son.'

Eventually I go over to Peter's and his ma answers the door.

'He's in the room, Collie. Ah think he's been fightin'. He's coverin' his eye wi' a bandage. Ye's never learn, dae ye's? Always gettin' intae fights wi' other boys. Ah'm tellin' ye, boy, whit ye's need is a nice lassie. Aye, that wid sober ye's up, eh? Payin rent an' a job tae dae?'

Peter pulls away the bandage. He's been slashed from the hairline, down through his eye.

'Jesus! What the fuck happened?'

His reply sends a chill down my spine. 'Albert. Wee Joe came up tae the door. My ma gave him tea, and he asks how you're doin'. Collie, I wisnae thinkin'. When I went tae meet you, they came walkin' into the Howf. Albert didn't say anything when Ah said Ah didnae know where you were. Then when Ah walked oot, they're there waiting for me. Fuck, check the eye: it was that wee bastard Mulligan. Albert looked fuckin' bonkers – ye know what he's fuckin' like, Collie.'

CHAPTER NINE

●

'**C**OLLIE! THAT** mob's at the fuckin' front door!'

Whit the fuck . . . ? Hammy's panicking: Eileen and I are in his house for a smoke. This isn't supposed to happen. Albert, Wee Joe, and another guy are at the front door. Hammy's handing me a commando knife: he's white with fear, this isn't his scene, the violence.

Johnny's his pal: he's been in the gang but has turned into a hippy, the long hair, the beads. 'Why are ye's aw fightin', man? Fuck, man, we were aw pals. Ye's should aw drap acid, man. Fuck, man.' He's taking the horrors. 'Go oot the windae! Fuck! Hurry up!'

There's a forty-foot drop: if I break my legs, they'll leave me in some mess. A few days ago they slashed Peter through the eye. I'm right in trouble. What the fuck do I do?

Hammy's back in the bedroom. 'Collie, Collie, it's okay! It's just Wee Joe and Daft Reggie! Gimme back the blade. Nae trouble, okay, man?'

Eileen is ashen and shaking. She knows the score. Peter was done because he wouldn't give them my address. I've got an open razor in my back pocket. Eileen gets our coats and things together: she knows I'll do him, and that excites her.

'You lookin' fur me?'

Wee Joe is playing with a kitchen fork. He's not tooled up, the bampot. 'Aye, I'm supposed to be.'

My hand's in my back pocket, on the open razor. 'Well, here I am.'

Wee Joe flies at me. A lamp goes over. He's stuck the fork in my head. I'm pulling his hair back, my legs around him. I hear the zipping noises: *zip, zip, zip, zip.* Four long cuts down his face. He's struggling to get away, blood splashing onto the walls.

Hammy's screaming, 'For fuck's sake, no! For fuck's sake, no!'

I've four tiny holes in my scalp, a joke compared to his face. My fingers are sliced open, but I've done the wee bastard: I've left his face like a railway crossing, the fucking bampot! Hammy's got the commando knife and we're all standing in the kitchen. Wee Joe's holding a towel to his face; we're both covered in blood, it's everywhere.

'Where're ye gaun fur stitches?'

I don't want to go to the same hospital because the coppers all know we're fighting and they'd tipple who'd done him. Hammy freaks out: he looks as though he's set one of us up. He stabs me in the shoulder: I try to grab his arm and ram the nut on him. Wee Joe tries to grab a kitchen knife, but Eileen slams him full in the face with a leather bag. Blood splashes out everywhere. Hammy's a junkie: this isn't his game, he's just in a panic. I don't touch him.

Reggie's in the hall.

'Who the fuck are you, stupid?'

He's chalk-white and stammers that he's just the driver.

I hold the razor at his throat. 'Right then, driver. Drive us tae the Garngad.'

Big Peter's delighted. His eye's a mess, it's ruined his looks.

'Ye got that wee bastard?'

I'm on a high, too, describing the fight in detail.

'C'mon, Peter, let's catch them one at a time. Do the fucking lot of them!

Peter's all for it, but first there'll be a pint; he can't do anything without a pint. Eileen thinks his bottle's crashed, but he's my pal, and I know he'll be okay.

● Saturday night: Sauchiehall Street's busy, pubs closing, people on their way home. I feel stoned and I'm dying to get up the road, get something to eat first. Eileen's tired, too, so we'll just get a carry-out and roll a couple of joints, have a quiet night for a change. Fuck, I hate walking when I'm stoned, the road never seems to end. The Yellow Bird: aye, we'll just get fish and chips and then a taxi.

Thunk! What the fuck . . . ? Wee Joe's face is coming out of a doorway and two other guys – one's his brother. I see the flash of the butcher's cleaver before it hits me, full force, along the jaw bone. My back teeth crunch and break as I hear the *thunk* in my ear. 'Ya bastard! I'm falling back, twisting away, hair drooping down my coat. He's swinging a meat cleaver at me again, but this time he's missed.

He's off now, running to a car. I'm on my feet and after them, grabbing two bottles from a guy as I pass: I put them through the back window, but the car speeds away. Bastards! I touch the tip of my chin. Fucking pricks! The gash keeps opening, all the way up behind my ear. I don't feel pain but the blood's pouring out of me, steaming-hot blood running down into my shoes. Eileen's screaming. Taxi-drivers refuse to take me; a bus-driver pulls me on and doesn't stop for other fares. I feel sick but manage to stay on my feet until we reach the Royal Infirmary.

● Saturday night is busy. 'Er, I've been mugged, nurse.' I'm wheeled into Casualty. When I ask the doctor how many stitches I'm getting, he doesn't answer directly.

'You're very lucky, Mr Collins. Had the cut been straight across, you wouldn't have been getting any stitches.'

My da and Peter are standing by my bed; Eileen's been there all night. I look like the mummy from a film, and Peter's in hysterics. There's a bandage wrapped around me like a woollen scarf, with my top lip and teeth sticking over the top. Peter puts a cigarette up my nostril. Fuck you!

I look at my da. 'Get me a gun. I'm going to do every one of those bastards.'

I can't believe his reply: 'Ye'll have to screw the nut, Hughie.'

What? I'm lying here with ninety-odd stitches, and he's telling me to behave. What's happened to the hard man?

The coppers arrive – Broken Nose and some other guy. They know the score but still ask for a statement.

'Bovver boys. They mugged me. I was drunk. I don't know what they looked like.' Statement over.

'Well, well!' They smile. 'And we thought it was your wee pal, Mulligan. Imagine that, eh? Bovver boys.'

Eileen gets clothes and I sign myself out. I decide to lie low for a few months until my beard conceals the scar. My swollen jaw eventually goes down and I take out the stitches myself some weeks later. The scar runs the length of my jaw but can be hidden. I tell people that the cut was a joke, just a wee nick.

● Peter and I are walking down Springburn Road. We're both carrying blades, steak knives, in our rolled-up newspapers. I've got a new hide-out, just a bedsit.

'Don't give anyone the address, Peter, no matter who.'

I know he won't, but the paranoia is ripping out of me. Peter is paranoid, too, so we're always on the look-out: you never know the minute.

'Here, check!' Mulligan's brother and that other fuckin' bampot – they're both going into the dole office. 'C'mon, Peter!'

'What? What the fuck are ye gonnae dae?'

I'm at the door of the office: there are long queues, people waiting to sign on. I spot them.

'Right, Peter. Catch them if they come out the other door.'

Peter thinks I'm kidding. 'Are ye aff yer fuckin' head, man?'

He's standing there, looking at me. I slip the blade from the newspaper as I walk up behind them. *Smack! Smack!* Their heads open up like melons. Blood splashes on my hand; I drop my arm and quickly walk out. They don't even know what's happened. People are confused by all the commotion.

'Mah fuckin' head's cut! Mah fuckin' head!'

Peter's laughing at the whole thing. 'Nae cunt even noticed ye!'

My heart's racing. 'C'mon, Peter, keep walking. Quick – grab that taxi!

We head off to a pub in Byres Road. I can't stop laughing.

'Did ye hear him? "Mah fuckin' head's cut! Mah fuckin' head!" The fuckin' bampots, eh?'

● The door to our flat has been kicked in. Fuck, I only left twenty minutes ago to get cigarettes. There's a bolt embedded in the pillow on my bed: Albert has a crossbow. Only half an hour ago Eileen had come to collect me, and I'd jagged up some morphine for a hit. They missed me by minutes. My stomach churns with fear at the thought. Eileen blames Peter for giving them the address; we gather some things together and leave. Later I find out that Mulligan's sister, whose flat was directly across the street, had seen me standing at the window. They thought I'd realized and bolted when they arrived. Jesus, that was close!

● I'm holding Lynn in my arms at the bus stop; Eileen and I are taking the wean to Eileen's sister. The stop is next to spare ground at the corner of Royston Road and Springburn Road; after the traffic lights a few yards ahead, the road peters out into flyovers and roundabouts. I see a bus coming down Springburn Road: it's ours, thank God.

'Lynn, ye're a big lassie noo! Ye weigh a ton, pal!'

She's giggling away but refuses to get down.

'Collie, look! Albert and Mulligan!' Eileen panics. 'Oh, God, the wean, Collie!'

Albert is racing ahead of the others, trying to beat the bus:

there's a meat cleaver in his hand. My heart's pounding. The bus slows to a halt just yards ahead of him. I leap on behind Eileen and the wean; they fall into a seat beside an old woman.

I pull a flick-knife on the driver. 'Fuckin' move! Get the fuckin' boot down! I'm fuckin' warnin ye, move!'

Lynn's screaming. Albert's running alongside the bus, trying to knock in the automatic doors, battering them with the cleaver. His face disappears from view. We're out of danger.

● I'm on a bus, going to meet Peter. It's always quiet on Sunday mornings, never see anyone around. Peter wants to meet me over at the Glasgow City Art Gallery: he's probably been tripping because then he likes to go to the gallery, walking round and looking at the paintings. I'll be bored out of my mind, and I hate all those stupid attendants looking at me. Peter's eye isn't too bad now; they stitched him up well, considering he was cut through the eyelid. The scar will fade to a wee line. Those fucking traffic lights, they're every two yards, every time you want to ... *Crash*! The whole window in front of me has fallen in: something's gone through the roof of the bus. Jesus Christ! The three other people on the bus are shocked too.

'Whit the hell wis that?'

Albert's standing by a billboard, laughing his head off: he has a crossbow. Mad bastard. He's too far from their car to come after the bus; he's too busy laughing, anyway. Fucking crazy bastard! They know it will attract too much attention to come after me. That mad fucking bastard! Did he aim at me or did he try to miss? Something will happen eventually, but did he do that just for a laugh? I know what he's like, he'd do that just to see what happened. We're almost at Kelvingrove, a passenger's still shaking his head.

'Bloody vandals, eh? It's bloody terrible.'

'Aye, should lock 'em up.' I agree. 'Terrible, eh?'

Jesus.

*

● All Peter thinks about is sex. We're up to our eyes in trouble, and he's out again with another bird. He says he wants to get Wee Joe, but I don't think he's serious: I'm on my own.

Fuck. There they are. Albert, Wee Joe and two other guys. They haven't spotted me. With a hammer in my coat pocket I follow them all over Glasgow, pub after pub, in and out. They're probably looking for me. One of the guys is Albert's brother. Looks like they're heading home – if I could just catch one of them by surprise . . . I wish they'd split up. I'm freezing, creeping round after them. Albert's taking them to his house. I'll hide in the back close with the light out, and wait for Wee Joe to leave. Fuck's sake, what are they doing in there? I hear voices on the stair above. I'll hide in the midden. Oh, fuck! The rubbish bins are full: potato peelings, ashes – they're stinking. I'm crouched behind them, covered in fucking rubbish. Someone's in the back court. I clutch the hammer. He's walking towards the midden: is it one of them? I come flying out, swinging the hammer. *Thump!* I strike something as a full bucket of rubbish hits me in the face. The guy staggers back in fright as I clamber over him, straight into a washing-line at neck level. I'm thrown on to my back as the rope catches under my chin. Oooph! Fuck, the hammer's gone! The guy who'd thrown his rubbish is yelling, 'Help! Help! Get the polis! Help! Help!'

Aw, shut the fuck up.

Lights are going on, windows are opening. 'Whit the bloody hell's goin' on doon there?'

I beat it back to Peter's. His ma lets me into the house.

'Fur the luv a God! Where hiv ye bin, boy? Peter! Look who's here – and whit a sight!'

● Eileen and I are staying at a friend's house overlooking a loch; Lynn is with us for the weekend. I'm up early and standing at the window.

'Eileen, get the sean ready and I'll take her over to the loch.'

When I turn back, someone is parking a car at the front of

the close: Albert, Wee Joe and two other guys are getting out. Albert has a brand-new double-barrelled shotgun. I can't believe my eyes. I pull the wean into the bedroom; Eileen doesn't have to be told who it is. I grab a hammer. Albert's coming in the back close just as I reach the bedroom door. The letter-box is rattling. I squeeze through the narrow gap in the window and run up the next close, my mind racing. What should I do? I run back into the street and smash some windows: within seconds the street is heaving with people. Sure as fuck, they come running out: Albert has a coat over his head, concealing the gun, while Wee Joe brazens it out. They speed off in the car.

Later in the day I manage to get hold of a sawn-off shotgun. My da's pals have given me the run-around but eventually I have a gun and five cartridges. I love the feeling of having a gun, secure. Now we'll see who's fucking who! I keep the gun under the bed at night but play with it on my own, pretending to swing round and pull the trigger. Click! This evens things out: no more running away. I don't give two fucks what happens, as long as I get one of them. Click! The gun's easily concealed under a long leather coat. I walk up and down the living-room, trying it out: yes, you can't see it till it's out, stuck in your face. Click! I wonder what it's like, being shot. I'm dying to fire it and see what happens. I love the feeling of it under my coat. You just swing around and up it comes. Here, Albert! Fuck you! Click!

● I'm snowballing on coke and smack, high but levelled out – a good, clear stone. Eileen's high, too; we're both flying. Albert has challenged me to a square-go. He knows that I have a shotgun: he's put it to me that it'll be just me and him, with guns, hatchets, blades, whatever I want. He's not shy, is he? What about a bazooka, then? Albert scares me, though. I know how fit he is, and how determined. I'm high, I have a shotgun, so fuck him: I'll go whatever way he wants. I'm going to fucking shoot him: fuck him! But I'm scared. I know I'm scared: no one else does.

The George Hotel is jam-packed. The pubs are closed on Sundays, so the hotel lounge is heaving. The Bear is sitting at a table. There are about eight of them: 'Whit's happenin', Collie?'

I'm feeling okay: the gun's inside my coat. I've cut through the coat pocket, my finger's on the trigger, my palm's sweaty. Where's Albert and Wee Joe?

The Bear has no part in the trouble, but he likes to do his promoter. 'Collie! Albert's been lifted fur daen a turn. Aye, he's dun fur armed robbery, him an' two guys frae Manchester.'

The Bear's pal is trying to look heavy. I don't like the way he's looking at me: I'll put him right in his place, the prick.

'Well, if anybody wants trouble . . .' I pull my coat back and raise the gun. 'Any fuckin' one of . . .'

Boom! A black swarm hits the roof. The sound is deafening. People literally jump with fright. The fucking gun's jumped, too; I'm on the floor trying to find it. I'm deafened, my neck's burning. Where the fuck's Eileen? The Bear's crouched over, covering his ears; his pals are on the floor; everybody's too stunned by the noise to make a move. Eileen's in hysterics as we run into a lane; we're both laughing like mad.

'Fuck! Did ye hear that fuckin' noise? Boom! Ah thought it wis a fuckin' bomb!'

Albert is in jail: he gets twelve years. I'm frankly relieved. Wee Joe and the others will collapse without him, he's the driving force. Twelve years is a bit heavy, though. I'd have been with him on that robbery and doing a twelve right now with him: we did everything together. I should chib Jack Cousins for causing all this. Albert has fallen out with me before, but not like this. Fuck, we are like brothers, closer to each other than to our own families; even Wee Joe and the Bear are like brothers. And now all this – what happened?

Rumours are flying round about the shotgun. Collie fired a gun in the George! Collie fired a gun at a guy! Collie held a gun at a guy's head and the trigger jammed! Oh, yes, I tried to shoot a guy but the gun jammed – it's always the same story. Now the coppers know that I have a gun and they're looking for me, but that's no problem: I don't need it now, I'll put it out of the way.

● The Burns Howf is a mixed attraction. The upper floor houses progressive rock bands, and the long-hairs hang out there. The ground floor is the main bar, where the Rod Stewart look-alikes drink: they buy one drink and pose all night, all flash and no cash, the straights alongside the modified long-hairs. We're there, drinking. I'm looking for hash and meet two brothers selling it. I know them: they're okay and need money. There's no problem for me, just two guys grafting. Peter's eyeing up a bird and I go upstairs to the toilet to do the deal. Then there's one brother holding a blade at my throat while the other goes through my pockets for money.

'Bread, man! We need the bread!'

Junkie bastards! I'm raging but I can't move; the bastard behind me has me by the hair and I don't even have a blade. The cubicle door crashes open and Peter's standing there, a look of disbelief on his face and a blade handle sticking out of his waistband. Thank fuck. I stab the first one in the face. The blade hits teeth. I stab the other one in the stomach and the hand. We're off, but Peter gets stuck between the two fire doors.

The brothers are in the lounge now, screaming. I walk down the stairs, passing the Drug Squad: they're looking for me but don't recognize me. At the main entrance a bouncer tries to stop me: I've been set up. I batter him against the wall and walk into the darkness of the street. Some time later I'm taken to an identification parade: surprise, surprise, it's the two brothers, two brothers on an innocent night out . . .

Drugs have produced a new type: grasses seeking criminal compensation, criminal injury money, free cash. All they have to do is finger you, get you convicted and they get the pay. It's a fucking rip-off.

They have to convict you, though: if they don't, then they don't get a penny.

● I'm out having a drink with Peter. Peter's relieved that Albert's away, and I don't blame him. We're having a blether about our faces. Peter's eye is healing but his good looks have been spoiled; his head's been fucked up with it all. Albert's really put fear into him; Peter sees him everywhere, in the streets, pubs, clubs . . .

'Peter! For fuck's sake he's in the jail. Twelve years!'

Nothing will convince him. As I'm talking, I see a guy coming into the bar: he's the fucking driver! He was there when I copped it with the cleaver. I can't believe my luck.

'Right, Peter. Swally that pint. C'mon!'

Peter has an open razor.

'Geez that! Draw that prick oot tae the front door. It's Stu Brown, one of that fuckin' mob.'

Peter walks over to the bar as I slip out; the guy doesn't recognize me with a beard. The pub has stairs outside the door, and I hide below them, waiting. I hear voices above me: the guy is leaning against the stair rail with his back to me. Peter's eyes widen as I emerge . . . Zip! I pull his hair back and rip him open from his chin to his scalp. The guy screams out as I jump down into the passage; he's still shouting as I'm halfway down the street. 'Ya fuckin' bastards! I'll fuckin' get ye back, ye bastards!'

But he's a guy I've never heard of: Jinxy, a professional boxer who does hash and cocaine. He's a chibman, a heavy guy. This is the guy I've slashed: the wrong guy. Jesus Christ.

CHAPTER TEN

●

AT THIS PERIOD, for the first time in my life, I was seeing
my father regularly. History and chance had conspired
to keep both of us out of prison. He was living a ten-
minute bus ride away. But I didn't like what I saw.

Once I was at some awful club – everyone in platform shoes
and three-piece suits – when I was tapped on the shoulder: there
was an old man at the door asking for me.

An old man? I didn't know any old men. I went to the door
and discovered my father, covered in blood. He'd been done
over and come to me for help. His face had been slashed and he
didn't have his dentures in. His hair was long and messy, and his
clothes smelt of drink and piss.

My father: the old man.

I took him home in a taxi. I cleaned him up and discovered
who'd slashed him. When he was in bed, I went out and stabbed
the guy who'd done it. I assured my father that the guy would
no longer be a problem.

He wasn't. But the next week, late, there was a knock on the
door. It was my father: the puckered face without its dentures,
the hair, the blood, the soiled clothes, the smells. And so the
routine: I brought him inside, cleaned him up, asked him who

did it, then went out and did the guy. Every time it happened, I duly went out into the night and chibbed someone (except for a black guy whose flat I broke into, ready to stab him as well, when I came across an old-fashioned iron and used that instead: I learned later that he was in Intensive Care with a cracked skull).

● Peter and I are drinking in town. There's a party later and he's keen to go, but I don't really feel like it.

'Eileen's expecting me back early, Peter, so you go on yer own, okay?'

Peter flips his lid; he pulls a razor and starts mouthing off. 'Back early? Whit the fuck's happenin' wi' you, man? Eileen's fucked things up wi' us. She's fucked yer head right up wi' aw this fuckin' shite.'

I'm watching the razor in his hand. Peter's freaking out more and more often on acid, but that's no excuse. One wrong move and I'll take the face off him, no matter how close we are. I finger the blade up my sleeve but the moment's gone, he's not going to try anything. I turn my back on him and walk away. I'll see him tomorrow when he's sober.

Eileen's pissed off: Wullie and Ginty are at our place, steaming drunk. My old man and his bird. I'm tired of him fucking things up: breaking furniture, spraying beer all over the place, repeating in his drunken slur that I'm his boy, his boy the chib man, his fucking boy. I suspect that he's just allowing himself to get into trouble, knowing full well that his boy will sort it out. It's as if he's now living off my reputation – or, more frighteningly, living through me.

They're drunk all right. The beer's sprayed on to the walls, the place is sodden with booze.

'There's yer boy, Wullie!'

Ginty, a prostitute he picks up every night after she's done her graft, has a battered, swollen face, wears a tartan mini-skirt and white plastic boots. How anyone could want sex with her, let alone pay for it, is a mystery. She's a young woman but already aged through physical abuse. My da thinks it's a big laugh. He can wake her up in the morning just by opening a can of Calrsberg Special. She lives on cans of lager, unable to sustain a diet of regular food. Wullie – the hard man, the big hero, grafting skin – can't even look after the source of the booze habit.

Peter arrives at the front door. He denies everything he said earlier in town. I'm too stoned to be bothered. Eileen is stoned, too. The television's blaring in the corner, drowning out the drunken rabble.

Big hero wants to know what his boy's doing. 'Whit's that fuckin' stuff yer smokin'?'

Shit, he knocks the hash all over the floor. Everyone's laughing. It's all a big laugh. Yes, let's have a laugh, a real big laugh.

I jam my shotgun in Peter's mouth. 'Right! Get fuckin' stripped!' Peter's eyes are bulging. 'C'mon, get fuckin' stripped!'

Eileen's turned on by the danger; she's giggling as she watches the show. Peter's jeans are at his knees, he's panic-stricken, desperately trying to say something . . .

Big hero's pulling at the gun – and I hit him. For the first time. I smack him across the forehead with the gun butt, pulling back both hammers of the loaded barrels, aiming directly at his face.

I'm within a muscle's twitch of blowing my father away. He's lying there in the recess, his flies undone, genitals hanging out, his hard, scarred face in a spasm of fear.

I see him for the first time in my life – see him for what he is. My father is not the hard man. The hard man is a lie. Robin Hood? He is a drunk, poncing money from a burnt-out prostitute half his age. He is not the man I wanted to be. What I wanted to be has been a lie. It didn't exist.

But just look at what the lie has created.

CHAPTER ELEVEN

●

I KNEW WILLIAM Mooney, the man I murdered. I didn't like him, but I didn't like a lot of people. In any case, it's not the reason I murdered him. There was no reason to murder him.

Mooney was a big man, about my age, and weighed fourteen or fifteen stone: stocky, but fit. He had quite a reputation – he was from a gang called the Peg – but I didn't meet him until 1968. We were both at the Young Offenders' unit in Barlinnie. He was on his way out, and I was settling in to serve an eighteen-month sentence. I held to my father's principles, and didn't talk to screws or act friendly to them in any way, so Mooney's attitude was bound to irritate me. He was a screws' pet, making them tea and doing them little favours. The day before he was due to be liberated, we had an argument. I suspect I resented that he was about to walk free – that he'd probably got parole because he got on so well with the screws – whereas I was on my way to serving my full sentence, down to the last possible minute. I offered him a square-go, but he wasn't having any of it; after all, he'd be having a pint with his friends by the same time the next day. I then went to the screws and asked if Mooney and I could have a square-go. They almost always obliged, leaving the two of you alone in a room and only intervening if the fighting got out of hand. But the screws told me to fuck off – they knew Mooney would be beaten. I drifted back into the television room and then went to bed.

At Barlinnie the cells are unlocked at six fifteen on the dot, but the next morning they were unlocked at six. I had been asleep and opened my eyes to see Mooney rushing through my cell door, coming at me with a steel bar. He hammered my nose with it, then pulled a blanket over me, picked up the steel washing basin nearby and slammed it repeatedly on my head. He went on to pound my joints, one after the other: one shoulder, then the other, the elbows, the spine, the pelvis, the knees. Then he left, closing the door behind him. I couldn't follow, even if I'd been able to: I was locked in. In fact, I could hardly walk.

Fifteen minutes later, Mooney was free.

● I didn't see him again until the day I killed him.

Wee Joe had asked to see me. With Albert in prison, the rest of them had folded. They wanted to square things up with me, get back to earning money again. I met him in the George Hotel. His face looked like a road map, which pleased me. 'Ye don't look too bad yersel',' he commented, meaning the scar he'd given me, although without open hostility. He asked if I could score some dope for Johnny Gemmell. Johnny was in prison, and he was due to visit him the following day. There was no trust between us now, but I did like Johnny. I told him that I'd meet him later, around seven o'clock, at the Lunar Seven: 'I'll get some blaw an' we can see where we want tae go frae here, okay?'

With Wee Joe was Mooney (Mooney, I learned later, was seeing Wee Joe's sister, and Wee Joe, the Bear and Mooney were a sort of gang within a gang). I hadn't come upon Mooney in nearly ten years, and while I hadn't forgotten the beating, I was willing to let it pass.

Wee Joe went off, and I joined Mooney for a drink. Mooney was already half pissed and in a boisterous mood. Two women were with him and he was showing off a bit. He wanted to do things: shoplifting or thieving. He asked if I'd help him slash a guy; he said there was money in it and that in any case the guy was a mug. I agreed, mainly to keep Mooney happy, although I thought that he'd been watching too many gangster movies. He kept jabbering away. He had a round, innocent face with a turned-up nose and a permanent half-smile while he talked, leaning into your face. He suggested that we all head off to one of the women's flats as the pub was closing.

Along the way, we ran into a nephew of mine. He was with his mates, a gang called the Pickpockets, and Mooney decided to have a go at him. The Pickpockets was one of Glasgow's best-organized gangs. It had about a dozen members, all young – between the ages of twelve and sixteen – and all dedicated to making money. They avoided violence; they were thieves, especially adept at stealing jewellery. They travelled regularly – they'd been in Switzerland the week before – and always had cash. They could also be remarkably generous: if you stepped in front of a copper during a chase, they'd make a point of rewarding you later, as much as three hundred quid. But they didn't respond to bullying, and Mooney was bullying them: he wanted money.

I think I would have objected to the bullying anyway. The fact that its object was my fourteen-year-old nephew – who couldn't fight sleep, let alone a fifteen-stone, body-building maniac in a half-drunken state – meant that I was bound to get involved. And so it happened. Mooney pulled out a bread knife, threatening my nephew. I told him to leave it out, and he turned on me instead. 'I'll give it to you again,' he said.

It seemed that Mooney, too, hadn't forgotten the beating. In the circumstances, it wasn't going to take much to provoke me; this was certainly enough. And I told him so: I told Mooney to meet me at the Lunar Seven that evening. Then I'd be tooled up, and we could go for a walk. By now I was extremely angry, and my nephew, who, a moment before, I was protecting, stepped between us to calm things down.

● Wee Pate and Felix Reilly came into the Hunting Lodge in Sauchiehall Street, looking serious.

'We've been every fuckin' where lookin' fur ye! That mob's tooled up, Collie!'

'That mob' were Mulligan, the Bear and all those other clowns who thought that they were now in a gang – total bampots, messenger boys.

'Mooney's wi' them in the Lunar Seven. They're settin' ye up, Collie, so don't go near the fuckin' place!'

They explained that I would be invited to a party in a high-rise flat and, once there, would be thrown over the veranda.

'They're plannin' tae fill ye wi' acid tae make it look like an accident. Mooney wis mouthin' that he wis gonnae tan ye, an' that's when it came oot – so jist gie them a bodyswerve.'

Felix suggested waiting for them outside and catching them when they were all drunk – he'd tanned a few of the Tongs that way – but I couldn't face going through all that again. I couldn't face the fear again: shotguns being produced in front of the wean, Eileen terrified out of her wits all the time, my own paranoia . . . Fuck it, I decided.

I thanked Wee Pate for marking my card and let him go – he had nothing to do with this. In my bag I had a brand-new Bowie knife with a twelve-inch blade, and Felix had a blade on him, so we decided he'd be there beside Mulligan when I arrived. We agreed that I'd do Mulligan if they invited me to a party.

'Right, Collie. Don't get stoned, okay? We'll weigh in a few of them. See ye later, pal.'

There was something crazy about Felix. He'd even stabbed a guy in the prison chapel, but in all the time I'd known him, I'd never heard him swear. He as always quietly polite: 'Yes, Hugh, let's slash this chap for being rude to us.'

When Eileen arrived, I put her in the picture. She didn't say anything – probably too stoned. I loved her and her daughter but I couldn't shake off this trouble. It had to be tackled once and for all. Eileen carried the blade in case the coppers pulled me on the way to the Lunar Seven.

My stomach was tightening into a ball. Sauchiehall Street was busy, lots of people about, some already drunk. I was seeing the Lunar Seven in my mind: the place would be dark, except for the bar. Where would they be standing? At the back, probably, next to the side exit. At the Lunar Seven the exit is through a swing-door, down some stairs and then out onto a lane. Eileen passed me the blade without a word. I slipped it up my sleeve, handle first for convenience and speed in the event of a fight.

As we walked into the pub I was aware of everything – the noise, the shadows, the smell of cigarettes and beer, faces turning towards me, knowing glances. I spotted Felix, next to Mulligan by the bar.

'Collie!' shouted the Bear, arm outstretched. 'O'er here! Wit are yes drinkin'?'

They were all wearing coats and drinking tomato juice: no alcohol. I moved to stand beside Wee Joe. The scars on his face, like four railway tracks running down it, still looked raw from when I'd chibbed him.

'Hiv ye got the dope?' he asked.

'Aye, I'll gie ye it in a minute.'

Mooney brushed past me: I ignored him, but was aware of his every move. Eileen was with Felix behind me as I looked over my shoulder; when I turned back to the company, a tumbler flew past my head and coming towards me was Mooney. Suddenly bottles were flying everywhere, birds were screaming. The knife was in my hand and I plunged it into Mooney's chest just as he reached me. I could feel the material of his jacket against my knuckles from the force of the blow, and I knew I'd done him.

'Collie, he's dead! Walk out quietly,' said Felix in my ear. He tried to pull my arms back. 'C'mon. Walk away.'

But Mooney was trying to pull a bread knife from inside his coat, staggering towards me. Something snapped inside my head. A part of my mind detached itself, watching: over the rest I had no control. Even if I'd wanted to stop myself, I couldn't have resisted the overwhelming urge to savage the guy.

I grabbed Mooney's arm and pulled it upwards, exposing his ribs, and plunged the blade in between them with all my strength. Fuck you! Fuck you! Fuck you! I pulled out the knife and rammed it in again.

But Mooney had me by the hair and threw me against the exit: down we went, Mooney clinging to my hair, my blade in his ribs. Bottles were smashing around my head. Mooney's blood was all over me. We hit the landing and he was astride me. He had a beer tumbler in his hand, lifted it in the air and smashed it against the side of my head. I yanked the knife out and plunged it upwards, into his throat.

I could hear distorted voices, see faces floating past me. The physical effort left me on the ground, spent, as though there'd been some emotional ejaculation. I got to my feet, covered in steaming blood, the knife still in my hand. Mooney swayed, made a gurgling sound, and slid down the wall. Then it hit me. I'd gone berserk. I felt like a monster.

What the fuck have I done?

Staggering, dazed, I saw him die in front of me.

● I heard sirens and moved away, turned down the lane and dropped the blade into a dustbin. I found myself in a fish-and-chip shop. People were staring: no one said a word about the blood. I was covered from head to toe in it. What was I doing there? I didn't want to eat. A few minutes later I was standing at the corner opposite the Lunar Seven. It was cordoned off, with coppers standing in a circle, but I could see Mooney's feet sticking out.

On the late bus home there wasn't a sound: a packed bus but not a word spoken. Eyes avoided mine as I looked around.

'Whit the fuck are ye all lookin' at?'

Silence.

At home I stripped naked and pulled out the shotgun. I loaded it and sat behind the front door. When the coppers came, it would be over for once and for all. I sat there until dawn.

CHAPTER TWELVE

WHEN I CAME out of my daze, I cleaned up and took the clothing and the shotgun to the woman next door. She hid them in her loft and then ordered a taxi for me. I wanted to get to a safe house where I could contact my old man. Gypsy Winning, my da's pal, came to collect me. He'd been involved in a murder, (and was later murdered himself) but for the time being he would know what to do. On the way to the safe house, he suggested that I rob a bank while I was still on the loose.

'They'll dae ye anyway, son. I'd fire straight intae a bank. Ye're talkin' aboot a lifer, so dae as much damage as ye can before they get a haud of ye.'

When my old man arrived, he just looked at me. 'Ye're in bother, eh, Hughie? We'll have tae think this through.'

I'd never asked him for help before. When I was just a boy he'd said to me, 'Dae whatever ye want, son, but don't ever come runnin' tae me greetin' if ye get done fur somethin'.' Now he wasn't in any position to help at all, not really: the coppers would be onto him right away. He didn't look the hard man now; he looked worried, and sad. 'Ah'm takin' ye tae the Big Yin's, so get ready. He's over in Partick.'

No one asked any questions when we arrived. Collie Beattie, the Big Yin, said he'd help, but first his wife and son would arrange a meeting with Eileen. 'Now, Mither will make you something to eat, then you'll see you're wee girlfriend before you go to America.'

His presence was overpowering. I managed to nod my head and force down some food while they talked. His wife tried to put me at ease, but for some reason I couldn't look her in the eye. I felt like a murderer.

The Big Yin's wife and son left to meet Eileen: the Big Yin and my da went out to meet a guy in a pub. Hours passed. They returned, reassured me that everything was all right and left again. I waited and waited. Something had definitely gone wrong. My da reappeared on his own. No sooner had he opened his mouth than *bang*! The front door was ripped off at the hinges and there were coppers everywhere. The bastards had been watching and waiting . . . They pulled me over the couch by the hair, turning my face to identify the scar, and wrenched my arms straight up my back: 'Identify yourself!' My da immediately stated that he was in charge of the house, to protect the Big Yin's family from prosecution on the grounds of harbouring a wanted murderer.

As I was being rushed out, I shouted, 'Da! I'm not resisting arrest! Remember that, okay?'

Four detectives drove me down into a tunnel. I could barely breathe, squashed between two of them in the back seat. They stopped the car somewhere: it was pitch-black outside, no street lights, just darkness. The two in the front leaned over. 'Where's the shotgun? We turned yer hoose o'er, Hughie!'

The coppers either side of me were pressing into my ribs. 'Where's the fuckin' shooter?'

'Fuck off!'

One of them pressed a handgun against my temple, and opened the passenger door nearest me. 'Go ahead, gangster. Have a go. I'll blow ye'r fuckin' brains out!'

My stomach was in knots, but I laughed at him.

'Who dae ye think ye's are? The fuckin' Sweeney? Ye've no got the bottle tae fire that thing, ya fuckin' bampot. Go on then, fuckin' fire it, ya fuckin' prick!'

'Right. Get this fuckin' animal doon tae the station and charge him wi' the murder of William Mooney.'

On the way they tried a softer approach, asking personal questions.

'Why'd ye no just shoot him, Hughie? Ah mean, ye's aw had guns, didn't ye's?'

My head was reeling with visions of jail. Fuck. A life sentence. The thought turned my stomach upside down. Jesus, I'll never see Eileen and Lynn. I'll never see anyone again . . .

'By the way, whit did ye dae wi' the blade? Just sling it, Hughie? Well, it makes nae difference tae us, like, an' ye're no gonnae tell us anyway, so it disnae matter really. It's just out of interest, ye know? Dae ye want a smoke, Hughie?'

● After I was formally charged at the station, I was put in a cage for observation. A copper came to have an informal talk about the situation, 'just a wee chat'. I knew him quite well – Broken Nose, one of the old heavy mob, the quick-response division, the Untouchables.

'Well, well, Hughie. Trouble this time, eh?' He put his cards on the table. 'Right. We've got that lot up the stairs with Eileen. They're being charged with harbouring you. It's quite a serious charge, so it's not a tale to get you talking or any of that nonsense, okay?'

I said nothing, but my heart was sinking. I was worried about this kind of pressure on other people.

'Now, look, we know the score. You all fell out with each other – it was on the cards. We've been waiting for one of you to kill another. We know there have been guns involved, but we can't prove any of that. Fair enough? Okay so far, Hughie?'

My mind was racing. There had to be a way out of this for Eileen and the others. I said nothing.

'Mooney had a blade, so it could have been you lying in the mortuary. That's fair enough. But what we need is the blade you used. So let's work something out. I'll come back later to see if we can do a deal.'

I was only concerned about my da's friends. I looked at him, and decided there and then. 'Okay. Let them all go and I'll gie ye the blade.'

Right away they drove me to the lane. A detective said that it had already been searched on the night of the murder, three days ago. I was able to pull the knife out of the dustbin, caked in hard blood – so much for the detective work.

The knife was put into a plastic bag for forensic tests, and I was taken back to the station for further questioning. I had a fifty–fifty chance – Mooney had been found with a blade, hadn't he? I felt that I had done the right thing for my da and his friends, and also Eileen.

'Well, Hughie. That lot have gone home now. No charges have been brought against any of them.' It was Broken Nose. 'Eileen's father has been very cooperative. That's how we got onto them, you know. He let us tap his telephone, and we simply followed Eileen.'

I felt wounded. Eileen had let us all walk into a set-up? No, I don't believe this. She wouldn't do that to me ... She had, though. I was destroyed. Eileen later pointed to me from the witness box during the trial and said, 'Yes. He is extremely violent.' Her evidence tore me apart because she was the only woman I'd ever loved and trusted. Her betrayal had a far worse effect on me than the life sentence. I felt deeply injured for a long time.

The following day I was taken to court. No plea or declaration was made on my behalf, and I was remanded in custody in Barlinnie Prison, pending trial for murder.

CHAPTER THIRTEEN

I WAS HELD ON the ground floor of the 'untried' wing. All the capital charges were kept there, locked up for twenty-three hours a day with one hour's exercise and a fifteen-minute slop-out period. Prison clothes were kept outside the cell doors after lock-up to reduce the risks of suicide and escape. The place was full of headcases.

I discovered that the Bear was in the hospital wing, as protection from other prisoners – and from me. Apparently he had handed himself in on the night of the murder, stating that he had thrown a bottle but that I had done the stabbing. Grassed from the word go. His bird had made a statement as well.

It didn't surprise me that Joe Mulligan had also made a statement against me. I had suspected that he was a police informer for a long time. He just couldn't handle jail, so he played a double game, chibbing some people and grassing others. A fucking maggot. What a fucking mob, I thought; they want to chib people, but when there's retaliation, they run to the coppers. I swore to myself that I'd kill Wee Joe the first chance I got at him.

(Later he was caught with another guy's bird, seemingly on

the game. Her boyfriend had waited in the bedroom with a couple of pals, and when Wee Joe went to bed they came at him from the wardrobe and the recesses, swinging iron bars. Mulligan lost an eye and had a steel plate put in his head, but he'd managed to scrawl the guys' names in blood on the bedroom wall, so he grassed them too.)

While I was awaiting trial, three further charges, of attempted murder, were brought against me by the two brothers who'd tried to rip me off in Burns's Howf and the guy I'd done in Sauchiehall Street. Fuck me! I couldn't believe this – attempted murders? I'm the one who was fucking mugged and they're charging me for retaliating?

In June I'm taken to court to appear in an identification parade concerning the charges. It's a couple of days before my twenty-sixth birthday and I'm standing there in the line wondering where this is all going. I had already spent about ten years in jail and now more loomed ahead. These new charges would almost definitely blow any chances of being found not proven on the murder. Bastards!

The first of the brothers was escorted in by a copper and pointed me out without the slightest hesitation. When the second one came swaggering straight over to me I banged him square on the jaw: 'Fuck you, ya fuckin' grass!'

The coppers were on top of me immediately, shouting about even more charges, for assault, but I didn't care. I had wiped the smirk off that fucker's face. Fuck you! C'mon, charge me! C'mon, go ahead!

Back in the cell things began to hit me. This wasn't the fucking movies. This was a real live nightmare – I could spend the rest of my life in prison. I had never felt so trapped in my whole life. Something crazy was bound to happen: suicide was on my mind all the time, it seemed to be the only way out of this. Oh, Jesus, please, please let me wake up and find that this has all been a bad dream.

*

● Felix had been lifted. I spotted him in the yard and we grabbed each other. He said he'd help me in any way possible, even in an escape, so I began to give that a lot of thought. A few days later I came up with an idea that I put to Felix in the exercise period; he thought it was too dangerous but eventually agreed to help.

I outlined the plan to Peter Blackburn when he came to visit the following day. He was worried but said he'd do what he could.

'Just bring clothes and a message' – he knew I meant a gun – 'to the Royal Infirmary on Saturday. Leave the lot in the toilet, and get out before ye're spotted, okay?'

On the Thursday I managed to smuggle a glass mirror into my cell. After lock-up I snapped it into three pieces: one looked like a dagger, perfect. I wrapped spare socks to make a rough handle, and tied it tightly with a strip of blanket, then lay on the board to wait for morning.

During the exercise period on Friday I slipped it to Felix. He was anxious. 'We're still friends, aren't we?'

I felt agitated and scared. 'Felix, just fuckin' dae it, will ye? I don't gie a fuck what happens, okay?'

Five minutes before the exercise period ended, we slipped past the screws through the hall and down to a storage cell on the ground floor. We waited for the prisoners to be herded into the hall, and when I heard their shouts and noise on the stairs I leaned over a locker, my back to Felix.

'Right. Go ahead.'

Felix shook my hand – 'We're pals, Collie' – then plunged the mirror-dagger into my back. My left leg jerked upward with the shock. Felix had to be pushed out of the cell. I waited for a few minutes until the main body of men had passed on their way out of the hall and Felix had closed his cell door before emerging.

I put my fingers to the wound. Blood was running down the back of my legs in a sticky stream. I staggered to the screw's desk, and when I told him I'd been stabbed he shouted for an immediate lock-up. Then I passed out. I briefly came to on the ground outside the hall, with an old screw asking how I was, and the next thing I knew I was on a huge table in the prison surgery, surrounded by screws.

'Who stabbed you?'

'You're dying. Who stabbed you?'

'Right. Get him to the Royal Infirmary. He's a capital charge – double-escort.'

The double escort discussed golf and overtime, as usual, on the drive to the hospital. When I'd been stitched I could hardly move, but I knew I'd be all right the next day. I just had to wait and rely on Peter to play his part.

I woke up to find myself surrounded by staring screws. Some prick had grassed.

My Uncle Shug came to visit me. He told me that my aunt, who worked in the hospital, had been warned that a prisoner was planning to escape, that he was dangerous and not to be approached, that the police had guns. The prisoner was me.

The senior screw tried to offer me advice. I knew him from the Young Offenders' unit, one of the heavy mob, a bully, 'Look, Hughie, don't do anything daft, son. Yer goin' straight to the Special Unit as soon as ye're sentenced. Boyle's there, he'll help you get sorted out.'

I felt so frustrated I could hardly spit out the words. 'Fuck you and the fuckin' unit, ya prick.'

Dangerous? Guns? Special Unit? Who the fuck did they think I was – John fucking Dillinger?

When they were taking me back to Barlinnie I was dressed in a smock and plastic slippers and handcuffed behind my back. From then on I was isolated from the others, exercised on my own and considered a high security risk. Whenever I was taken anywhere in the prison, I was handcuffed and escorted by four screws. I'd suddenly become dangerous. It was a strange feeling, gave me a sense of power, separated me from the population. It made me special.

*

● Courts are places of intimidation. You can smell the fear emanating from the dock, the fear of authority. I feel no different from anyone else on trial, fear trembling below the surface, every fibre alive with apprehension. Breathing irregularly, suffocating.

The jury returns a verdict of guilty on the murder of Wullie Mooney. All the other charges against me are not proven. Wee Joe's face sneers from the public gallery. The Bear's and Wee Joe's evidence convicted me. I'll kill those two bastards. I'll fucking kill them stone-dead.

The judge is addressing me, but I don't hear the words. Only when he pronounces sentence do I catch the flow – '. . . do sentence you to life.'

I turn to the two arresting detectives behind me. I spit in one's face, 'Fuck you!' I lunge towards the prosecutor to attack him. The police escort on either side drag me back and downstairs. Bastards! Bastards! Bastards!

Life imprisonment. My stomach flips, the way it does in an elevator that suddenly stops unexpectedly. My legs almost give way with the sudden heave of shock.

● Tony, the guy with the nose hooked like a claw hammer, looks at me through the bars of the cell.

'How'd ye get on, Shug?'

I've done the first thirty seconds of a life sentence. What do you say to someone who asks how long? I'm suddenly embarrassed and flustered.

'Er . . . life, Tony.'

'Well, let's get the cards out. We're short of a hand for five-card brag.'

CHAPTER FOURTEEN

———————————————————●———————————————————

I'M LYING FACE down on the floor as my eyes open in the dimly lit dungeon. I've been battered unconscious by prison staff: their riot sticks have left splinters of wood wedged in my scalp. The blood has congealed in some places, in others it's still oozing. Insects are crawling all over my hair and body, but I can't bear to move.

The dungeon lies directly beneath the hall. They threw me over the rail of a spiral staircase in the centre of the hall, and as I lay at the bottom I could see them all jammed on the stairs in their eagerness to get down, with their sticks.

Some time later I hear them coming down again, shouting, steel toe-capped boots clattering on the stone stairs, keys and chains clanking against the narrow walls. The noise of their approach is more terrifying than the beating I'm expecting. The cell's steel door crashes against the wall as it's thrown open; they pour in, brandishing their riot sticks. The cell is filled with screws and sticks. I'm being spreadeagled, they're jumping on my spine, kicking me all over. Noises and flashes of light explode in my head. I literally see stars as the blows rain down. I can hear them grunting and swearing as they push each other aside to get at me, accidentally striking each other. I bite a hand before my vision doubles and I black out.

The following morning I have to lever myself up the wall to get on my feet as I hear them coming down the stairs. It must be about six, so I know it will start again. They try to open the door quietly, but when they see me in the corner they just charge at me. The only thing I can do is spit, so for a few seconds I keep spitting in their faces and call them all the bastards of the day. They really do me over this time.

Later in the morning the prison doctor arrives to examine me. I'm being held up by two screws and a third one smashes his stick over my head. The doctor says nothing. The cell is going round and round like a hallucination as I'm painfully injected with some drug. The doctor tentatively uses his stethoscope but more screws squeeze into the cell swinging their riot sticks, and he scurries away. I hear another stick breaking over my head and crunching noises in my skull as I lose consciousness.

The prison staff kick the shit out of me twice a day for five days solid. My body turns black with bruises and seems to swell to three times its normal size. Their boots have left streaks of polish on me, and there are insects everywhere, moving or dead. The pain in my whole being is unbearable: moving one muscle sends a searing pain through my entire body. I can't see properly, I can't focus.

The beatings stop. I'm handcuffed behind my back, my feet are cuffed together and I'm heaved into a prison van, face down on the floor. The van is crammed with screws, digging their boots into me, pinning me to the oily metal.

The destination turns out to be a hospital. They warn me not to open my mouth. Someone frees my feet and my arms are gripped as they rush me through the doors, past staring faces, all in a blur.

There's a heated dispute between the doctor and the screws. He demands that the handcuffs be removed; they are adamant that the handcuffs stay on. The young nurse who steadies me on the X-ray table is asking questions about my appearance; she sounds upset by the attitude of the screws. I discover that I have two broken ribs, lacerations on my scalp requiring twenty-eight stitches, ruptured testicles and bruising from head to toe. My skull is fractured.

On returning to prison I find the hall packed with screws. They line every landing, hanging over the rails to stare at me. The screws on the ground floor are very menacing: they spit in my face, growling, 'You fucking scum! You're a fucking animal!' But no one physically assaults me. The escort rushes me down the spiral staircase and into the dungeon. I'm in the hole in the ground, totally breathless but somehow relieved. The cell looks worse than before; there is shit all over the floor and the smell is terrible. Images of people and events are flashing through my brain: a screw on his knees pissing on the polished floor, his whimpers as I stab him again and again, his hairpiece coming away in my hand. Have I killed him? Should I feel some sort of remorse? The fact is that I have enjoyed stabbing him, every blow sheer pleasure.

I hear the door open and clang shut again. There is a plastic bowl on the floor, filled with an odd mixture of food: soup, custard, cabbage, cake, potatoes, carrots – all in the one bowl. I pull myself over to the nearest corner, scooping handfuls of food into my mouth; at least it's warm and offers a kind of comfort. The food is making me feel much better – but something is wrong: I'm swallowing something that isn't mushy like the rest of it. Instinctively I gag and throw up all over myself, and there it is, a dead mouse, already flattened with decay. I throw the bowl at the door: a fucking rodent in my mouth, a fucking dead thing. Bastards. If I come out of this, I'm going to kill one of them.

Later I lapse into sleep, motionless on the floor, looking into the darkness until it covers me. I'm seeing an ocean, breathing with it as it swells, seeing its greenness, drifting with its endless motion. Suddenly I'm being dragged to my feet. Am I dreaming?

There are four screws in white coats, hurrying me into a leather restraint belt with handcuffs attached to the front. My hands are secured. Am I for the state mental hospital? No one is speaking. My hair is wrenched back and cloth is stuffed down my throat. I'm thrown on the floor, gagging as my head hits the wall. I'm pulling and straining at the handcuffs in sheer panic; there are spots where my eyes should be and my ears are filled with a rushing sound. I keep pulling until one handcuff's stitching bursts, and I can wrench the cloth from my mouth. I gulp air into my lungs in sobbing, breathless panting: my jaws seem to be stretched wide open, my whole head about ready to burst like a balloon.

I stay there on my knees, panting and sobbing until my voice screams out. The scream is coming from somewhere inside me, a very painful sound, the sound of deep fear.

● In solitary confinement there is no human contact whatsoever. The isolation is absolute. There is no sense of reality, only the intervals: daily exercise periods, meals. At Perth there was one other dungeon in the basement, and that was where I 'exercised' in an atmosphere of mutual hostility. A screw stood in each corner of the cell, watching me walk up and down, handcuffed and covered in my single grey blanket. No one spoke.

Food was passed in through the hatch of the cell door. Sometimes the screws would spit in it as I watched, but I just crammed it into my mouth without displaying any sign of nausea. That made the screws themselves squeamish; like schoolboys pulling a prank, they whispered outside the door, 'Fuck! He's eating it! Euch!'

The total absence of human contact would produce an actual physical pain, an ache. When I was forced to run the gauntlet of perhaps fifty screws to see a solicitor or a psychiatrist, I'd suddenly leap at the most hostile face just to feel the body of another person, a moment's relief. I would try to humiliate a screw by kissing him full on the mouth or forcing my tongue in his ear, shouting, 'C'mon, ya big darlin'! Ye're fuckin' dyin' for it!' This had more effect than a punch, and it made a screw reluctant to claim criminal compensation for being assaulted, which was a common method of paying for a new car or a holiday.

I lived like this for over a year, rarely communicating except through forms of violence. As the external world disintegrated, I lost myself in memories, living like a ghost among images that I could see but that never saw me. The accumulation of my experiences are what I have become: these memories are Hugh Collins. So I deliberately summon up an image and look at every detail, listen to every sound, relive the sensations they evoke and cling to every response, whether of love or fear.

● My heart accelerates as I see the image of Granny Collins, sweating over the cooker. The kitchen is hot, full of steam, chips frying and crackling, fish in the pan – I can smell them. Jack and Cathie will be home from work soon. Jack's shaving gear is in a cup sitting on a shelf above the boiler. There's a jar of Brylcream and a packet of blue Gillette razor blades. He looks like Cliff Richard in his Italian mohair suits and pointed shoes. Everything is immaculately pressed, down to his white, starched collar and black-and-red slim-Jim tie. My granny says, 'Put the plates out, son,' and a warm feeling of belonging floods through my body as I remember that. The plates are on the corner wash-boiler, next to the deep sinks with the terrifying clothes wringer attached to the wood between them.

When Alex and I were being scrubbed in the sinks, my granny would pretend that she was going to put us through the rollers to make sure we were dried properly. Shrieks of terror would invariably end in a quick skelp across the backside. 'C'mon, you pair. Get tae bed and nae carry-on.'

My granny almost fills the narrow passage with her huge bum and enormous breasts. I can smell her as I pass, a familiar, comforting, working woman's smell. Her blue apron with a pattern of small red flowers has a huge pin holding it together at the shoulder. She has on her old blue dress, which sways from side to side as she walks. She's wearing her small, black, zip-up boots with embroidered sides. Behind her is the grate where we sometimes sit at night, among the clothes draped to dry, listening to Cathie recount the story of the film she's just seen.

● A noise startles me: it's the screws, bursting into laughter. I look at the door with its garish green paint, at the peeling plastered walls, at the cold stone floor. My legs are numb. Those fucking screws are on my door round the clock, whispering all night. They get on my nerves. All they talk about is golf, the social club, promotion, overtime money, new cars and each other's wives.

They say there's a cell being built for me in Peterhead prison, a secure unit where I'll be kept away from other prisoners in unlimited solitary confinement. They hope I'll be given fifteen years when I'm sentenced. I've already been told that I'll serve at least fifteen years of the life sentence, so another fifteen won't make much difference. I know in my heart that I'll never last that long. Something will happen and in one abrupt moment it will end, in violence or an overdose. Thinking about the future, existence outside this cell, is beyond me; it only brings on depression. (The psychiatrist provides drugs – whatever and whenever I want: Mandrax, Seconal, Tunal, dolly mixtures. Sometimes I'm out of it for weeks on end and can't remember where I am or what's happened. This numbness is preferable to the reality; it's like a vacation.) The screws are still talking. Apparently two of the screws I stabbed are still in hospital.

● Blades are easy to get in most prisons: I got hold of a turnip-cutter and a dagger (used in making nets) and put them down the front of my trousers one morning, then told the screw taking the breakfast round that I was reporting sick. I hadn't slept all night, my bed was soaked with sweat. For a second I wanted to back out of it, but I knew that sooner or later I would explode and probably injure another prisoner, which was the last thing I wanted. This was going to be one big bang, then I would let them finish me off. It would be painful but they wouldn't be able to smother up my death: my problems were solved. The door swung open and then I was on my way downstairs with the knives hidden in my waistband. Here we go, I thought, it's big-time. This would be the last time I'd walk over this place. Then all the things that had happened to me came back and churned up all the rage inside me. My whole body was shaking with nerves. I could sense the screw escorting me; he seemed to be right up against me as I walked along the short corridor while he closed the door to the surgery behind us. Prisoners were milling around in the waiting room, and I stood with them, starting to get the knives out. Someone said, 'Here's the screw! Watch it!'

That first one, he puts up a real fight. His face when he sees me, two knives tied to my hands. He can't believe his eyes until he feels the first blow. I stab him seven times. The turnip-cutter splits his hat in two, the small ensignia of the crown goes flying, a silver button follows. His face is filled with confusion, fear, rage: he doesn't know why he's been attacked, and nor do I. I seem to explode and can't stop.

Prisoners are panicking, about twenty of them, caught in the middle of it all in the doctor's surgery, running and shouting. Then I hear the homosexual's voice behind me, like a woman's, squealing, 'What's all this bloody noise?'

MacLeod: he's the screw I want. The other one simply walked in at the wrong time, and now he's squirming underneath me. I stab at him with everything I have, then break away. MacLeod is trapped inside the prison surgery, the door is locked and he'll have to pass me. The turnip-cutter has broken, the handle dangling from the string around my wrist. The other knife is securely tied inside my balled fist as I pull myself up and move towards him.

'What's bloody going on?' MacLeod is confused by all the commotion, then suddenly sees me coming at him, shouting something. He collapses onto his knees, trying to crawl away from me, crying it wasn't his fault. I've never felt so much hatred for a person in my whole life. The polished floor is slippery with urine and blood. I'm astride him, pulling at the back of his hair, plunging the knife into his neck, blood spurting on to my shirt. His hair is coming away in my hand. Fuck! He's wearing a hairpiece. I've scalped him!

Someone has grabbed me round the neck from behind, a third screw. MacLeod's white medic's coat is splotched with blood. I keep trying to stab him as he crawls away but I'm being dragged backwards. I stab the knife into the screw's right thigh. The riot bell is ringing and ringing; it's deafening. I stick the knife into his hand and twist until we finally fall backwards through the door into the doctor's room. I feel the arm letting go and stab him twice more in the thigh as I clamber free. They are all lying on the floor, there's blood everywhere, spattering the walls and floor.

I hear shouts and boots clattering. I tear my clothes off and pour a huge container of medicine all over my hair and body: I'm greased from head to toe. I'm shaking with exhilaration and fear as the screws come charging in: they have shields and long riot sticks. I'm battered senseless as the surgery fills with more and more screws. I'm being run across a yard, carried spread-eagled towards C Hall, screws running at me from every direction. I'm being kicked in the face, battered with sticks as consciousness fades and returns: it's like slow motion with flashes of light and noises like colours. I'm thrown over the rail, down the spiral staircase. I'm looking up at them, their puffing red faces distorted with rage and exertion. Stuck tight together, sticks clattering, they look like Keystone Cops. Seconds drag by and suddenly the knot of bodies breaks and they're on me, smashing me with their sticks and chains.

CHAPTER FIFTEEN

●

MONTHS HAVE PASSED, I don't know how long I've been in solitary. When I leave my cell, all the other prisoners are locked up in theirs. Moving me involves all the screws on shift duty. I'm handcuffed and dressed in huge, baggy pyjamas with blue and white stripes, and large canvas slippers.

There's a certain power attached to all this: the more security, the more powerful I become. I'm being treated as someone who needs to be chained, watched, guarded, as the most dangerous man in the prison, as the most dangerous prisoner in Scotland.

'You still have hope.'

I hear those words, but they don't mean anything. The Governor is talking to me. He wears glasses with thick, square, brown frames beneath his deer-stalker hat. His little grey moustache, ruddy complexion and whole manner is that of a military man. Green tartan tie, green-and-brown checked shirt, green raincoat, brown brogues, umbrella swinging like a baton. Two chief officers stand on either side of him, their caps trimmed with white braid along the peak; they have more silver buttons than the basic-grade screws, and white shirts instead of blue. Red granite faces. They stare at me. It's like a military parade minus the band playing.

I'm being taken to court on a charge of attempting to murder three prison officers. I'm put into the Dog Box in the reception area, where my clothes are lying on the narrow bench. It's sweltering in there and I'm drugged out of my mind. I have difficulty dressing and am barely presentable. When I'm handcuffed I see my reflection in a mirror: long hair and beard, a haggard face with black-ringed eyes. Fuck, is that me?

The police escort the prison van to Edinburgh High Court. I don't recognize any of the streets we pass through. I'm handcuffed between two screws; they must weigh about sixteen stones. The cuffs are cutting into my wrists. I can smell their cheap cologne and hear all the usual conversation: their whole boring lives. I wonder who the judge will be, and whether my father will be in court. He hasn't written. I enjoy the sensation of travelling, the slight swaying and the acceleration and slowing down. I hope the van crashes, kills all the bastards – but, alas, no.

The court is a huge, dull building with an archway and staircase. I'm hurried down a corridor where barristers and lawyers hang around. We're put in a waiting room and I'm handcuffed to a pillar. Coffee arrives for the screws and all their talk starts over again: golf, cars, more golf, more fucking cars, more fucking nonsense.

The barrister appointed to deal with my case has abandoned it. The solicitor talking to me is willing to represent me, but he needs certain facts; where the knives came from, who made them, names. He says he's putting forward a plea of mitigation for a more lenient sentence. Mitigation? I don't know what the word means. I tell him to just plead guilty, I'm not interested in leniency. He gives me an odd look and leaves.

My name is called. The courtroom is massive. Symbols of justice adorn each oak-panelled wall. Before me lies a huge table littered with papers and with water jugs at both ends. To the right is the witness box; to the left, the empty jury benches. The judge's bench is high up in front of me; two ushers stand on either side of it, dressed in the full regalia of red coats and white wigs. The Crown Prosecutor is looking at me; he wears a stiff white collar, pin-striped trousers, a black gown and a white wig. As he continues to stare, I recognize him as the prosecutor who told the court he wanted me off the streets. He convicted me of murder. I smile at him from the dock – yes, it's me again, you fucking prick. I stare him out, and he snorts his contempt.

A trumpet blares and an usher calls, 'All rise!'

The judge enters in his white wig and red gown. He looks directly at me from the bench through his horn-rimmed glasses. His expression seems impartial, his face flushed and soft-skinned. I'm handcuffed to two screws; six more are seated directly behind me, but for once I don't feel intimidated by the court.

The prosecutor describes me as highly dangerous. He describes the attack and produces photos of the wounds. Apparently MacLeod narrowly escaped being paralysed. He asks for a severer sentence. While the defence barrister describes my wounds and situation, I look over my shoulder towards the public benches. My father isn't in court. There's just a mass of staring faces, fucking voyeurs at a circus.

I'm stood up as the judge addresses me. He asks me if I have anything to say, but I answer, 'No'. He sounds sympathetic, concerned about my future. When he pronounces a seven-year sentence, the prosecutor drops his head in disgust.

'Bastard! Seven fuckin' years,' a screw mutters under his breath.

The screws are furious. On the way back to the prison, a fight breaks out in the van. The screw opposite me can't suppress his frustration and spits in my face. I stamp my feet into his groin and all hell breaks loose. They jump over seats to punch me, cutting my mouth. I'm restrained by the handcuffs and can only return verbal abuse. Bastards! Bastards! Bastards! I spit all over them and shout all the way back to the prison. Bastards! Bastards! Bastards!

When we arrive the Governor is waiting at the gates with his entourage. He comes marching over, and someone tells him the sentence. He says to me that there's still hope. I hear him talking. I'm being held by the arms, fingers digging into my flesh, forcing them behind my back.

'I'm going to fuckin' kill one of you people! I'm going to fuckin' get one of you bastards!'

The Governor steps back, confused and alarmed. 'Take him back to his cell and give him a shower and some clean clothes.'

● The next day they moved me upstairs to the ground floor, into a cleaner cell. It had a window with a steel grid. The cell next to me was occupied by Robert Moan, a multiple killer who'd escaped from Carstairs, the state mental hospital. I knew they had me down as a psycho, and I played the part when I wanted something. I used the carefully deranged look to put fear into the screws, knowing that it would provide space from the population as a whole. They simply couldn't afford to call my bluff – not after the stabbings. I might just be a psycho killer.

While I was in solitary, prisoners used to turn their radios up full blast whenever Talking Heads came on. Their song 'Psycho Killer' was popular at the time, and John Peel played it almost every night. Prisoners would shout my name and turn their radios until you could hear it all over Perth Prison. In 1994 I met the singer David Byrne at his photography exhibition at the Stills Gallery in Edinburgh. Caroline introduced us and we talked, but I don't think he fully grasped the significance of our meeting. For me it was a strange experience: seventeen years had passed since hearing that song at one of the worst periods of my life. What a boost it had given me, hearing those radios go up.

CHAPTER SIXTEEN

———————————●———————————

I'M LOOKING AT the steel door. This door is different, painted pale blue, a soft colour against the cold steel, almost soothing. The curtain conceals three sets of steel bars set in concrete: beyond them is a wall ringed with barbed wire and security cameras.

The Special Unit building sits within this wall, separating it from the main prison. On the other side of the wall are the main halls of the prison, surrounded by yet another wall and, again, a high perimeter fence ringed with wire and more security cameras – a prison within a prison.

Barlinnie Prison houses a male population, but this place had been used as a wing for women serving custodial sentences until it was eventually closed down: the purpose of the wall no doubt was to keep the men and women separated from each other. Now the building was being used to hold an average of five prisoners: there were ten cells, but these were never fully occupied. Some were used as makeshift studios or for storing things.

I register the shapes looming in the darkness: a bookcase running along the wall of the cell, a blank television set in the corner, the armchair opposite – dense black shapes, dark shadows.

As part of an experiment in rehabilitation the Special Unit permits prisoners to furnish and decorate the cells. Their families pay for the furniture but the basic idea is about responsibility – I mean, who in their right mind is going to smash up their own furniture?

My bare feet feel the texture of carpet, a warm, comfortable sensation on my skin, so unlike the cold surface of concrete slate.

Am I dreaming? No, it's real. Someone breaks the silence, clearing his throat. The sound's coming from the next cell: it's Jimmy Boyle.

Hasn't he been described as the most dangerous prisoner in Scotland? Larry Winters, too – hadn't he been branded as such before he died? Hadn't they both been regarded as no-hopers? What am I doing in this place? How have I finished up in here – a no-hoper?

The day had been a blur of faces and people talking, but I can't seem to focus on any one conversation. 'You're head's fucked up,' Jimmy's saying. 'You don't think you are, but you're completely fucked up. I know how you're feeling. It's all so confusing right now, but you can make it.'

The journey was amazing. One minute I was in isolation, and the next thing someone's showing me around the special unit. It's another lifer, Jim Lindsey: 'Aye, Collie, this is the pantry.'

I immediately see the knives scattered across the hot plate. Just hours before I'd had a body search for any concealed weapons: they thought I might have a razor in my anus. The bastards must have been winding me up, knowing I was being moved.

Jim's taking me outside to see the small garden, centred on the main part of the L-shaped yard.

'I'm the gardener. Not bad, eh?'

The flowers with their bright colours are stunning – they make me feel dirty. The tree has small green apples. There are no screws in sight but the security cameras are following our movements around the garden.

'Jimmy does his sculptures over here. They're good, eh? I like the fist best.' Some old tenement blocks form a wee circle next to the garden: the fist protrudes from the centre like a huge dick, sitting there on the plinth made from two cable drums.

'C'mon, I'll take ye upstairs. Ye're next door tae Jimmy. How dae ye feel, by the way? Ma heid was up ma arse when Ah first came here, but ye get used tae it after a while.'

'How long are ye doin anyway, Jim?' I ask.

'Oh, Ah've done twelve years before this sentence. This is ma second lifer, so who knows how long Ah'll dae this time?'

There's a screw wearing a white medic's coat in my cell when we get there. I almost double back, thinking he's searching the place or something. He's brushing the carpet.

'Hi, Collie. I'm fixing the telly, then that's you all set.'

There's a wire cable being rigged from the ceiling light, with a rough wooden block at the other end with a three-way socket attached.

'Don't switch yer lights off at night when yer closing yer door. That's yer mains fur the electricity, so always keep it on okay? How're ye doin, anyway? Ma name's Tam Anderson, Big Tam.'

Jim's explaining the philosophy of the place. Prisoners are not automatically punished for bad behaviour but encouraged to talk things through with the community. There is no punishment cell. Prisoners and staff work together, discussing everything at the weekly meeting. Special meetings can be called at any time by anyone in the event of a crisis, particularly a confrontation that could lead to a violent situation.

Screws sweeping out cells? Prisoners' gardens and sculpture? Community meetings and crisis meetings? What the fuck's this all about?

The Special Unit had come into existence following the abolition of the death penalty. Prison officers had found themselves unable to cope with the new generation of lifers: what is to stop a murderer from murdering again when he has nothing to lose? What does he get? Another life sentence? The cages, the brutal disciplinary regimes and long bouts of solitary confinement were not working.

The prison officers themselves advanced the idea of keeping the troublemakers together, out of the mainstream. Ken Murray, a prison officer, helped develop the concept of a community involving both prisoners and staff in which debate would have a more therapeutic effect than any of the methods tried so far in controlling violent prisoners. Joyce Laing, an art therapist, joined the community during its infancy, encouraging prisoners to express themselves through artistic channels. As a consequence of her efforts, a fund was created, providing art materials.

Visitors were encouraged to visit the Unit freely, enabling prisoners to rebuild relationships while also developing trust between themselves and the staff. This trust nurtured individual responsibility: people were held accountable for their personal behaviour within the community, including the Governor – any breach would result in a session in the 'Hot Seat'.

Prisoners were given access to a telephone to arrange visits and maintain regular communication with friends and family. There was no structured work routine other than the regular cleaning duties and prisoners could work out their own daily routine.

The unit had been opened in 1974 and, in Scotland at least, had never been long out of the news. There had been a steady run of stories in the tabloids about drugs, drink, and sex parties.

Larry Winters had died from an overdose of barbiturates just before I had arrived. Larry had been serving a lifer, plus he'd accumulated a further twenty-six years in various other sentences. He stood very little hope of ever being let out of prison. In the eyes of many, Larry's death was conclusive evidence of both the availability of drugs and the failure of this penal experiment. Much as society might like to see its murderers killed off, the idea isn't that the murderers should do it themselves.

The most famous member of the Unit was Jimmy Boyle. He'd

attacked prison officers in Inverness and been involved in the rioting there. While he was in the Unit, he was the subject of a television documentary and wrote a book about his experiences, *A Sense of Freedom*. Jimmy now lives in Edinburgh, drives a Rolls-Royce, and is a very successful wine merchant, specializing in vintage Champagnes. But in 1978, when I arrived at the unit, he was its undeniable leader.

● Another prisoner comes into my cell, introducing himself as Peter Campbell. He's serving double-life. Jim's smirk of contempt doesn't escape me when Peter invites me for a cup of tea in his cell. Peter looks like a madman. His eyes are dead. 'The Baby-faced Killer' the press called him: he was fifteen when he killed an old woman to buy his girlfriend an engagement ring. He later killed a prisoner in Saughton – literally stowed him under the bed after stabbing him to death. There was no apparent reason for the attack.

Peter's talking to me, but I have the feeling there's someone behind me all the time; his eyes are staring right through me. He's talking low and fast.

'Don't listen to any of them, Collie. Don't let them near yer visitors, 'cos they'll try to work on them too. They've been trying to get inside my head for years.'

Now he's standing by the door, calling, 'Aye, Collie, two sugars is it?'

He's back again, whispering. 'The Boss might be listening. Tell him fuck-all. He keeps diaries, ye know. Ye only have to cough an' he's in there, writing. Ken's his pal, the two of them plan everything together. Ken's trying to get him out – thinks he's changed.'

Peter's definitely bonkers but he's likeable. He has a weird view of the whole world and it's no wonder.

'Eighteen years I've been in, Collie. Eighteen long fuckin' years without sex. Dangerous prisoners? All I want to do is fuck women, whatever way they like, wherever they like. I'm not prejudiced, I'll shag anything, anywhere she wants. Nice cuppa, eh?'

There's no stopping the guy. I'm trying to find a way out of his cell, but he's relentless.

'The screws? Don't trust those bastards. They all want to be yer pal, then they put in snide reports. Another cuppa?'

● The yard seems massive with the garden and the space for the sculpture; there's even a small badminton court. I feel the security cameras following me, but that doesn't bother me at all – that I can walk on my own without screws is amazing. Oh, spoken too soon: here's one ambling in my direction.

'Hi, Collie, Ah'm Gerry Ryan. How're ye feelin'? I'm new here, too. Can't imagine what it must be like for ye.'

I feel tense being with him. I mean, what do I say? Oh, hi, Gerry! He's tense, too, I can feel it, but he's asking questions.

'Collie, can Ah ask ye somethin? Ye don't have tae answer, it's jist that as an officer it's important tae me, dae ye know whit Ah mean? Did Perth Prison staff try tae murder ye in the cells?'

What? I don't believe this! Who's he trying to kid? He's a fucking screw, isn't he? He knows what goes on.

'Well, ye're a screw, so ye'll know that, won't ye?'

Governor Thomson wants to see me in his office. He's telling me that in no circumstances will violence or drug abuse be tolerated in the Unit; any violations will result in an immediate transfer. This is more in line with what I'm accustomed to in prison: an arsehole in a suit. Apparently Thomson is the fifth governor they've had; his predecessors have suffered nervous breakdowns or simply walked out, unable to cope with group accountability. He's been posted here specifically to impose thirty-five rules on the community, the result of the inquiry into the death of Larry Winters. He's tense but controlled.

'I'm not here by choice, nor do I like violent prisoners, but I have to work in the place. Jimmy Boyle will show you around and no doubt explain the Unit's philosophy. The policy here is freedom and responsibility, but I'm determined that this won't be abused.'

Freedom and responsibility? This transfer, I remember, is to create a feeling of hope in me. I'm facing an eternity in prison. It's a living death sentence, and I haven't even served two years yet. Where's it all going?

● Jimmy's moving round next door; daylight's flooding my cell and it's morning again. The cells are being opened: 'Morning, Collie!' Jimmy's jogging round the yard. The pantry downstairs fills with screws, all wearing white lab coats, all friendly towards me.

'Mornin, Collie! Needin' a hand with the pantry? C'mon, let's get stuck in. Did ye get any sleep at all? Ach, ye'll get used tae things. Jimmy wis the same. He's developed a good work routine. Ah'm Malky, by the way, Malky McKenzie.'

Malky had been in the Young Offenders, but had never been involved in any of the staff brutality. I knew him but not on a personal level. He seems okay, and very friendly with Jimmy. They train together, doing weights and sparring.

'Get into a routine, Collie, that's the key to this place. Mad Peter been on yer ear yet? Peter's brand-new, sex-fuckin'-mad, though, a sex mechanic on legs. Betty's comin' tae see ye the night, but get yerself a bird – and other visitors.'

Jack, Charlie and Alex Collins have been regular visitors throughout the years of institutions; they look upon me as their youngest brother. Now I find I have family from all over wanting to visit, and their concern is overwhelming until it becomes clear why they want to visit. 'Which one's Jimmy Boyle?'

Shug Collins, my Uncle Hugh, makes an appearance wearing corduroy shoes, corduroy trousers, corduroy jacket . . . corduroy hair. He's fifty-two but that doesn't put him off the outfits: gold medallions, shades, platform heels, flares – and that fucking hair-do!

'Scotland's Most Dangerous Prisoners!' 'The Gilded Cage!'

'Killers in Luxury!' Headlines like these add the final touch of glamour. Yeah, man, that's the young brother. Jimmy Boyle? Ach, Jim's okay, man . . .

Shug brings a bird, a bleached blonde with a knitted hair-do like his. We're all sitting outside.

'Take her upstairs, Hughie!'

I'm being really macho. 'Okay, get stripped.' I'm lying on top of her but something's wrong. I can't get hard. She's grinding under me. 'Oh, don't stop, it's so big, oh, it hurts . . .' Jesus! What's happening? I'm freaking out with embarrassment. 'Oh, please, harder . . .'

I pull the jeans up.

'Right, you, fuckin' move! Get ready an' get out!'

She's terrified but doesn't say anything. Shug's talking but I don't hear the words. What the fuck's wrong with me? Am I homosexual? I have to get away.

'Shug, look, someone's called a special meeting. Ye'll have tae go.'

Later I'm walking up and down in the yard, still in a state of panic. Jimmy joins me. 'How's things? Good visit today?'

What did he just say? Jesus Christ, he knows! He's smirking at me! Why's he asking about the visit?

'Oh, I'm brand-new, Jimmy. Aye, great visit, aye, magic visit.'

'Ah saw the bird. Did ye fuck her?'

Jesus, no! He thinks I'm a poof! He knows! He knows! Try to act normal, that's it, relax, relax . . .

'The bird? Aye, Jimmy. Fuck, three times . . .'

'Is that right?' He's looking at me from the corner of his eye. 'Hmm, that's amazing. Most people have problems getting it up.'

I'm laughing hysterically by now. What? Can't get it up? The laughter's almost uncontrollable, the pure relief of being normal. Jimmy doesn't mock me.

'Collie, look, ye've been traumatized, almost in shock. Whit's happened is a normal reaction, a reality check.'

I feel better, but what if I'd had no one to talk to about this? I'd have done something stupid, freaked right out somehow.

'Would you have fucked her outside? No? Well, why do ye feel ye should now? Why do we all feel we have to be macho? Collie, learn to treat people as people. Isn't that what we're asking for here, to be treated as human beings?'

● My da brings people, too, pals from prison and from the criminal world, all wanting to know what happened in Perth; what happened with Wullie Mooney, what's happening with Jimmy.

Almost every day someone just appears, dragging me back into a nightmare, reliving my violent, bloody past – it's all getting too heavy. When Johnny turns up it's a relief. He has cocaine, smack and hash. Jimmy's trying to protect the place from drugs, he's pulling people to prevent incidents, but he's right, I'm fucked up. When Johnny leaves I'm high on a snowball of cocaine and smack, a concoction that creates a high intense enough to allow my feelings to erupt. I threaten to attack staff unless I'm immediately transferred to another prison, preferably to the worst prison.

'I'm gonny fuckin' kill one of you bastards! I fuckin' hate every fuckin' one of yes!'

What am I really asking for? I know what I'm expecting: punishment or solitary or a beating or the very transfer I'm demanding. What I get, though, is the 'Hot Seat', a meeting where I'm questioned by all of them, staff and prisoners. The meeting's resolution, however, is not to mete out punishment but to develop ways of supporting me through my difficulties.

What the fuck is going on?

The following day I drink a full bottle of whisky. I don't drink whisky and I've never had a whole bottle before. I'm totally drunk, swaying round in my cell. Jimmy presents himself at my door.

'Right, you, doon the fuckin' stairs.'

'Whit? Fuck you an' yer meetins!'

There's a brief scuffle as he gets me out. The Dutch courage is going a long way.

'Ah'm no fuckin' scared a you!'

Jimmy's luring me on. 'Well, c'mon then. That's right, c'mon, just me an' you' . . . straight into the meeting.

This time I'm not going to be interrogated. I'm spewing with rage, at everyone about everything: the prisoners for being such obsequious arse-lickers, the staff for being so intrusive and nosy, the endless visitors parading through the place as if it was a public zoo, and these endless stupid meetings every day, sometimes twice a day, sometimes even more.

I'm bundled up – I expect this – and put in my cell: but, again, not to be punished. I thought I would be. But, no: I'm put in my cell to sober up in peace.

I don't understand.

Jimmy's there again in the morning. 'How's the hangover?' He sees my gear packed in the corner. 'Ye plannin' on movin'?' He laughs. 'Collie, people have been waiting for all this to come pouring out. The Governor? Whit about him? Ach, forget him an' his fuckin' rules. This place is about supporting people through their problems, but we can't just get pissed every time things get tough.'

Has Jimmy changed? Lifers don't talk like this: his genuine commitment shames me into admission – I'm fucking people's chances, fucking things up for everybody, like some fucking arsehole.

'Collie, try to find out who ye are and whit's made ye this way. Don't play their game, ye're not an animal.'

I did try to change but it was a long, painful process. My emotions were like monsters ripping me apart; everything was always so confusing. At times I didn't know if I could get through it all or if I really wanted to. What would I have left if I didn't have my feelings, whether they were rage or hatred? The pressure was always with me: the hopelessness of my situation. The life sentence – it was a nightmare.

My ma, Jimmy, Malky and Ken bore the brunt of the rage and self-pity. I would never have survived those early years without their support. Through time, though, I learned how to defuse the destructiveness. I developed a thirst for survival.

———————————————————●———————————————————

CHAPTER SEVENTEEN

MALKY WANTS ME off drugs. My da brought me a load of downers, Tunal mostly, and I take four or five at a time. I open the capsules and swallow the powder straight: the effect is almost instantaneous. When I reach down to untie my boots I slump over and remain in the same position until morning.

Malky got suspicious when I seemed to be calm. He double-checked after lock-up and found me kneeling on the floor, hunched over. When I came to in the morning, he was sprawled across an armchair, watching the television news.

'Mornin'. Cuppa tea?'

The discovery of drugs usually results in an immediate transfer, but I've nowhere to go. I've petitioned the Secretary of State twice for a transfer; the Prison Department rejected both requests. Malky knows that a special meeting won't resolve this. What could the community do? Supervise my visitors? Punish me in some way? Lecture me in a meeting? Slap my wrist? Nothing would be effective.

The cell is warm but I'm shivering slightly. Malky is making tea; he knows where everything is. He quietly hums a tune to himself.

'How many sugars?'

Jimmy is jogging round the small yard; I can hear his heavy boots stamping against the flat tarmac. (It's very tiring going up and down hill when you leave prison, you've been so long on the flat.) I'm lying back on the sofa, smoking a cigarette; there's a cool draught on my neck from the window above my head. The bedside lamp gives the cell a warm, red glow. The huge fishing net draped across the ceiling mutes any noise; there's only a pleasant hum from the fridge in the corner. Jimmy passes below the cell window again. I haven't trained in a long time – too fond of the drugs.

Malky's puffing on his pipe, looking at the small library stacked on my shelves: Marx and Engels, Kant's *Critique*, volumes of Burns and socialist writings. My Grandfather Norrie left the books to my ma: impressive reading, but unopened.

My head's clearer after a few cigarettes; the drugs are still in my system, making me completely calm. I hate that sense of tension when my skin feels as thought it's stretched across my skull so tightly it might split; walking around with my insides twisted in knots, trying to pretend that everything's all right, trying to avoid conversations about how wonderful the Unit is.

Malky turns the television off and makes more tea. There's no tension between us, the silence is comfortable. He doesn't ask me how I am, he's just thinking things through in his own mind.

'Right, Collie, how dae we get ye through this? Whit are ye on anyway – downers? Dae ye read that stuff: Marx and Engels?'

'Naw, Malky, my ma brings them up. Makes me look intelligent, eh? Fuck, I'm lucky if I make it past nine o'clock, never mind reading books. Who else knows, by the way?'

'Just me. So, whit dae ye think? Whit aboot booze instead? Whisky?'

'Whit dae Ah think? Fuck knows.'

'Yer auld man disnae give a fuck aboot ye, Collie. He blanks the staff, an' all the carry on, as if *he* was doin' the time. You're fuckin' stuck here when he leaves. That's the reality.'

'Aw, c'mon, Malky, is this the fuckin' therapy?'

'Naw, naw, Collie, don't start that patter wi'me. I'm tellin' ye straight: ye're scared to turn yer back on those bampots. Jimmy won't let them pull him down a hole. Ye don't find him lyin' on the fuckin' floor, dae ye?'

'So fuckin' what? He's gettin' fuckin' parole.'

'Well, anyway, booze would be safer – at least we wouldn't have to worry about another fuckin' overdose. Jimmy deserves a chance, doesn't he? Anyway, see ye later, okay?'

Whisky? I never used to taste it, even, because of the smell. Malky's right, though: it's the lesser of two evils. What do I do? How will I handle things? I'll need to get into a routine: training and sparring, some yoga.

Joyce Laing, the art therapist, has supplied me with art materials. I'd like to paint but I don't know how. I'll take the material into my cell tonight and see what happens. Anyway, I don't have to show it to anyone. Joyce is a nice woman, but that arty mob are all bampots. I don't like any of them.

● Malky has been sitting in my cell all night, watching TV. He'll be wanting to have another talk before lock-up.

'Hi, Malky. Aw for fuck's sake, smell the place – you an' that fuckin pipe!'

'Oh, sorry. Whit's that? Are ye gonnae start paintin'?'

'Aye. Is there anything wrang wi' that?'

'Naw, that's good. Get things oot yer system. By the way, there's a message behind yer books. I'll get the empty in the mornin'.'

'A message? Whit are ye on aboot?'

'Whisky. Right, now geez the pills.'

'Whit? The pills? Aye, right, Malky, ye must be fuckin' kiddin'!'

'Naw, Collie, Ah'm fuckin' serious. Geez the fuckin' pills.'

I look behind the books and sure enough there's a bottle of whisky. Malky's deadly serious about the drugs. We're standing face to face, but he's determined. I've known him since I was a boy, in various jails, and he thinks more like cons than most cons.

'That's the deal. Nae mair drugs. Kill yerself somewhere else.'

'Aye, okay, okay. Jimmy deserves a chance, eh? Here, fuckin' take them.'

Malky puts the pills in a holdall. He lightens up a bit. I know he means well with his methods. It's radical, possibly wrong, but I can't refuse. He's too fucking wide – that's the truth.

Malky chuckles. 'Collie, I'm right. Ye'll see in time. This place is an island, ye know – Ah'm jist here to stop ye fallin' o'er the edge. Anyway, I'll take the bottle in the morning, okay? So night-night. Oh, by the way, fancy a work-out and some sparrin' tomorrow – or are ye too depressed?'

The mocking, patronizing tone is his style with everybody. Malky approaches people like that: 'Who are ye today then, Collie? Are we dangerous today or is it just an ordinary bad mood?' Nobody else talks to me that way, especially daft screws who hardly know me in any sense. Malky's a one-off. He doesn't give a fuck, especially for that mob in the Prison Department; he's totally against them and pro-Jimmy Boyle. Well, I suppose he's right: this place is a nursery, an adult nursery. Scotland's most dangerous prisoners. What a laugh! The newspapers use that tag to profit from crime: 'Scotland's Toughest Nursery' wouldn't sell papers, would it?

● Jesus, this stuff burns the throat. The Irn Bru kills the taste but it's horrible stuff. Why do people get into drink? I can feel it working, though. Think I'll put on some music. Aye, that's better. John Lennon's brilliant. Jesus, what do I do here? How do you start a painting? Fuck, I've run out of Irn Bru to kill the whisky. Ach, so what, I'm a man, I can do anything. Whoof! It's coming down my nose. Aye, man, that's brand-new. Fucking brilliant.

Aye, John, fuckin' right. Brand-new, eh, man? Shamrock, ya fuckin' bass! Aye, 'at's fuckin' right – fuckin' bampots the lot o' ye! Think Ah'll write a letter tae some cunt. Ma auld man's brand-new – auld Bullet Collins. Ten-fuckin'-stretch fur two stitches – two daft stitches! Ah mean, whit's it aw aboot, eh? Aw, here, whit aboot iss, eh? On ye go, John . . .

Ah, fuck. Ah'm fuckin' fed up wi' aw this. Ah want fuckin' oot. Ah'm sick a the jail – Ah'm always in jail. Jail, jail, jail: that's all Ah fuckin' know. Jesus, Ah feel sick wi' this stuff. The whole fuckin' room's spinnin', an lookit the sweat – Ah'm fuckin soakin. Bastards. Ah hate this place. They should let women stay the night – they know we're shaggin', the bastards. Ah jist want a job, that's all. A job an' a wee family. How the fuck did Ah end up here? Fuckin' slag bastards, Ah fuckin' hate them. Fifteen fuckin' years. Fifteen years an' that's if Ah'm lucky. Aw, Jesus, why? I wis okay when Ah wis a wee boy. God, why did ye let this happen tae me, eh? You know everythin', don't ye? Ye fuckin' knew Ah'd kill somebody. Eh, that's right, you fuckin' knew. Whit a mess. Why me, ya bastard, eh? Fuck you an' everybody else tae hell, ya bastards! Dae ye know somethin'? Ah'm fuckin glad, an' see the next cunt that says a word tae me – they're fuckin dead. Aye, that's right, stone-fuckin'-dead. Let's see this paint gear a minute . . . There ye go, a man's head. Here, hold it, that does look like a head. If Ah dae this . . . an' that . . . That's better. Here, that's me! Fuck, that's me in a cell, or ma soul when I've been battered. Where's they other boards? Ah'll dae mair painting . . .

The paint is splattered all over my cell. I strip myself naked, knocking jars of paint onto the carpet as I stagger around. I apply the paint with a piece of cloth, dabbing, rubbing, splashing at the boards in a blind frenzy. The blaring music in my head stirs my emotions into a physical onslaught, an unchecked attack, until I finally collapse on the floor in drunken oblivion. This is how I begin painting: deliberately getting out of control, releasing the demons, letting the monsters out of their cages.

Malky's sitting in the armchair when my eyes open. He's draped a clean towel over it, to avoid paint stains on his clothes, and has lined up all the boards. He's studying them intently, puffing on his pipe. My head feels as though it's clamped in a vice, and I feel sick.

'Jesus, Malky, any tea?'

Sounds more like a croak.

'Mornin'. Ye've been busy, eh? How's the hangover?'

I can only groan. Malky's really interested in the paintings. I can't believe the mess as I unstick my hair from some paint on the carpet and crawl onto the sofa. There are paint splashes everywhere. My memory of the previous night is vague. Did I actually dance and sing? I remember bits, but not the whole picture. Malky's staring at the grotesque forms on the boards, tortured figures bathed in black.

'Collie, these are good. Joyce'll go mad when she sees them! Put them on the walls downstairs. They're frightnin', ye know. Whit dae ye think o' them yersel?'

'Malky, look at the fuckin' state of the place!'

'Ach, so what? Are ye playin' at hoose or somethin'? These are brilliant. Get intae it every night, man. Ah'm tellin' ye, Collie, this'll get all the anger out. Fuck, Joyce will be delighted wi' these, honest! Show them tae Jimmy.'

'Ach, we'll see, Malky. Any tea, man?'

● Almost a year passes before anyone sees the paintings, dozens of them. I stack them under my bed. The paintings don't make me go to sleep. I don't paint for a few hours and then feel relaxed – the very opposite. I'm as tense as hell and mostly frustrated, but there's a perverse pleasure in it. I'm enjoying dragging all these things up to the surface, and yet it's never enough, somehow. Malky's always in my cell, looking under the bed.

'C'mon Collie, let's see whit ye've done.'

Sometimes I just sit and stare at them. What do they mean? I wonder if I'm going mad; I love them but I know they're crap. The technical shambles drives me crazy because I know I can do better. I feel I can improve them in some way, but how? The drink's no good either; I just fall about the place. Why did I start all this crap in the first place? I'm not an artist. I want to paint all the time but not these horrible figures, all this therapeutic rubbish.

Jimmy looks in a lot. He's become friendly with my ma – they're very close. Ken Murray too. Together they're trying hard to involve me in the politics of the Unit. I try to accept a role in the community, but reaching conclusions through debate hasn't been my way: violence has always been my approach to any problem. Now I'm being drawn into a very different arena, where people discuss problems in a group, and the community encourages the involvement of visitors. I recognize the strengths in this but staff and visitors go home at night. I've served two years, Jimmy has served almost twelve. People who have no idea of my fears continually compare our interests and commitment – these people infuriate me. Their phoney sensitivity and bogus intellect is insulting; their own commitment is merely fashionable, a new trend.

Jimmy has discovered a political platform to pour his energies into. That's his affair. What I resent is the process of cloning: Hugh Collins = Jimmy Boyle Mark Two. On the one hand I'm criticized for not doing as he does, on the other I'm criticized for emulating him. Jimmy himself is supportive, and I take on board his criticism. He's determined to show that he's changed, determined to get out. I've no argument with that, but somehow I feel that this business of change is itself a denial, that it merely scratches the surface of the issue.

When Jimmy sees the paintings, I feel embarrassed. They reflect, he says, his own feelings about confinement. His enthusiasm is infectious, though; it's what most people respond to on meeting him.

'Have you shown them to Joyce? I'm sure she'll be pleased. Why don't you hang them downstairs? The visitors will appreciate them, too, Collie.'

Jimmy's sculptures are dotted about the place – but my

paintings? He launches into the philosophy of the Unit, the whole idea of self-expression. He's relentless on that subject: that's what makes him tick.

'How's Betty doin'? Haven't seen her for a while. Ye haven't fallen out again, have ye? God, Collie, ye don't know how lucky ye are. I'd have loved my ma tae have seen me here before she died.'

'Aye, Ah know whit ye mean, Jimmy.'

'How's yer da, auld Wullie?'

I explain the difficulties with the visits. Jimmy appreciates the problems – like hospital visits, without the flowers. I dread having visits, especially now that I'm not taking any substances to give me confidence. It's a struggle to hold a conversation. My da talks for about five minutes then goes for a walk on the ground floor, pacing up and down until he leaves. He hates the fact that I've become friendly with the staff and involve myself in the progress of the place. Meeting new people is worse: my conversation is limited to talking about my past and internal politics – it's embarrassing. I feel tense and drained after almost every visit.

'C'mon, man, where's all that fight? Look at yourself – look inside and learn to channel all that energy. Pour it into creativity: write it all down on paper. Use the time constructively so that it doesn't use you. Yer auld da? How do you think he feels, seeing you in here? Collie, look, people don't understand. There'll always be someone waiting to kick your balls. Ye've just got to keep going regardless. Right: dae ye fancy a nice salad for tea?'

● What does Jimmy really know about my life? He knows nothing about me, or my relationship with my parents. How's yer ma? How's yer da? Fuck! I'm tired of this line!

They're still pulling me apart, even in adulthood, just as they did when I lived with my granny as a wean. God, I can still see them, fighting over me in the street. I'm naked but for a blanket, dragged frightened from bed, pulled this way and that. I can still smell my mother's perfume mingled with his drunken breath: their voices shouting, 'He's mine!' 'He's comin' wi' me!' Now I'm being torn between his criminal values and her socialist beliefs. I'm always caught in the middle, trying to please them both at the same time.

All this confusion. Jesus, how I long for the simplicity of my relationship with Albert. I made a terrible enemy and lost my most trusted friend.

The paintings? Yes, I'll hang them, nail them straight onto the walls. Thomson, the Governor, hates the art work: he'll have to look at mine every single day. Aye, Jimmy, I'll hang the paintings up. That's a good idea. These paintings depict my life, they are me, so fuck other people's opinions. This place is my life now. I'll paint, draw and write, write about everything – Jimmy's right. I have to fight back this way. My da will just have to accept that things have changed now. I can't lead a double life to please him any more. It's really that simple, so fuck his criminal codes.

What I find the most difficult in this new approach is the discipline. The daily training first thing in the morning, the daily sparring sessions, the whole routine of getting myself fit and working regularly. Malky's battering me every day now. He's a very powerful fourteen stone but I like fighting him. There's no holding back but no malice either – it's making me fitter physically and mentally. I'm feeling better being free of the substances but I have to fight the pangs, they're there all the time, creeping up on me – I rarely sleep at night.

I'm more aware of being locked in a cell, behind the steel door, with no escape, no escape from my own thoughts. The silence at night makes it impossible to escape from the images flooding my mind. I try to find distractions but I'm trapped by the deep fears of my own beliefs. I've felt the power of killing a man. I don't deny this but I'm haunted by the fact – I've killed a human being.

The prison authorities have simplified the whole question of remorse. They simply require an apology and good behaviour over a number of years. I'm sorry. I won't do it again. I promise this time.

Wullie Mooney battered me. I hated him. I feared him. Isn't that why I killed him? I can't lie about this. I killed him because I was afraid: he too had a blade, hadn't he? He had done me before. It seems the only logical explanation. Why, then, do I have all these conflicts? Why do I lie awake at night, confused? Why don't I just say, I killed him, big deal, so fucking what?

The Roman Catholic Church blesses soldiers going into war to kill: to kill people from another land, to kill men, women and children – there's no discrimination. God is on their side – whatever side happens to win.

Now, I'm a killer: I've done the thing that they do. I've taken a life. I won my battle but do I get blessed? Am I forgiven by the Church? Am I allowed to celebrate victory anniversaries? Was God on my fucking side?

No, I'm labelled and treated as a murderer. I'm locked up in prison for the rest of my life. I'm expected to make some sort of apology, tell lies to procure my freedom and forget about it, forget about murder. Being a Catholic complicates everything, though. It's not so easy to forget, especially when your actions contradict the basis of your beliefs. Oh, yes, I'm a believer. My brain looks logically at religion and scorns my naïvety, but in my heart lies the belief and the terror that it's all true, that there is indeed an afterlife, where my soul will be judged and cast into Hell.

This, I think, is where the confusion springs from – I killed a human being and for this there can be no forgiveness. I pray that there *might* be forgiveness, however. What I want to deny is the truth: the fact that I felt total power in killing someone, that sense of victory when you win. What's to stop me from killing again if there's no forgiveness? It poses a very real question to my mind: especially when there is the possibility of spending my life in prison, especially at night, lying in a concrete box, with all this shit running through my head.

● (In the Special Unit I almost became a Christian. There were respectable people who took me up, and they were born-again Christians. I played along with them, and it was like a poultice drawing out the poison. The people observing me saw the company I was keeping, and that was good for my record. But I was on heroin at the time, and when those people were praying in my cell I was not at all touched emotionally – and why should I have been? One of the things they petitioned God for was guidance in choosing a new car . . .)

● In the morning I'm dressed in a tracksuit and heavy boots by five thirty, waiting in the semi-darkness for the cells to be opened at six. Who am I today, I wonder? I jog round the yard, do weight training and yoga for a couple of hours before showering and having breakfast. I'm healthier and fitter than I've been in my whole life. People are describing this as survival; I call it completely bloody ironic.

I begin the day by writing on an old prison typewriter. I like the rat-tat-tat noise of the keys clacking like a burst of machine-gun fire, shooting as footsteps pass my cell door, rat-tat-tat. Why am I doing it? I hate writing. It takes me a whole day to type a single page, and I can barely spell without a dictionary. What I should be doing is sitting out in the yard enjoying the sunshine, or spending the day with visitors. I give the material to Jimmy: it might be taken away from me and it's best with him. But what I'm really looking for is his approval. I want to hear that he likes what I'm writing but don't have the nerve to ask him. Eventually I ask him what he thinks when we're watching television one night.

'Truthful?' he asks.

'Yes,' I say.

'It's fuckin' crazy.'

'Oh.' I try to explain that I come from a different generation, younger; it is bound to seem crazy.

'No, it's nothing to do with that. It's the writing. You jump all over the place. In one paragraph you're five, and in the next you're fifteen. It doesn't make any sense.'

My first composition lesson. I'm crushed.

I push myself on and start to keep a diary. I discover big words and neatness. I'll sit for hours trying to find a word with a certain number of letters so that the lines are absolutely even, with no hyphens. It's an obsession: nice, tidy, square paragraphs. I can't pronounce half the words I'm using in the text.

I develop a routine over the next six years that demands sixteen to eighteen hours' work a day. I write diaries, draw and paint. I take up stone-carving. I explore every aspect of my inner world and my external environment through the eyes of an artist. For once people are quite impressed with my achievements, but when I'm alone literary or artistic development becomes quite meaningless. It's one end of some spectrum of insanity that keeps me locked in the banal life of a fish-bowl, where I swim round and round, going nowhere indefinitely.

CHAPTER EIGHTEEN

─────────────────●─────────────────

NOVEMBER 1984. Six a.m. I love this time of day when everybody is still asleep. There's deep snow in the yard: I'll have to clear a path before I can do any jogging. The winter keeps people indoors, so I'll have peace to work without being watched. I can't explain why I'm doing sculpture – I'm just thankful I was given some encouragement by Jimmy. When I first began, though, I was just battering things out without any thought. It really was more like therapy, a method of getting rid of physical tension.

● The Christ statue was commissioned by St Columba's Church at the request of its then minister, Donald McDonald. He based the commission on a series of anatomical studies I had carved in stone the year before – a make-or-break project because I wasn't prepared to kid myself that I was a sculptor if they were crap. When Donald commissioned the statue for the church he had no guarantee that I could pull off a life-size figure. He simply took a chance and arranged for a stone to be lifted over the wall. Most of the art works could be sold to visitors, but this was different. This was my first time on a proper project, a public commission. I had never actually been asked to do anything like this before – and by a church at that. Was God on my side after all?

I bled on this stone, hands torn to shreds, working sixteen hours each and every day. I deprived myself of visitors to commit myself to the schedule, punishing my body, pushing myself physically beyond the limit. Was I simply trying to find forgiveness? Sculpture isn't about punishment or finding an inner peace, of course, but for a while I found a way of dealing with self-destruction through the work.

Michelangelo's work had provided a model, but how I wished I could understand the process. There's more to sculpture than a statue, a finished object, a thing. My Christ statue is a complete shambles. Technically I'm taking the form too far because I have to prove that I can carve all aspects of anatomy. My personality is stamped all over the stone. My ego prevents it from being beautiful; it has become mechanical. Jimmy and the others were slightly mocking when they saw the huge block of stone in its rough state, but I've shown my commitment, if nothing else, which is an achievement. The work itself – the actuality of the whole motion – is more important to me than the final object. This is where the true beauty lies, not in the shape of form.

Maybe I'm going mad, spending too much time on my own out there. I can't believe that it will be finished in just a few more months. I'll be really cool about it. Sculpture? Yeah, no problem.

● It's torture running round and round in the slush. The security camera is following me, and Bugsy, one of the warders, is laughing – no wonder. I feel like a hamster going round. The statue's looking good in the security floodlights, the frost like diamonds on its surface. Today I'm doing the right forearm and the hand. The yoga is making me feel better, but this is definitely unhinged. I'd prefer to be in a warm bed but I don't have the time.

I do have the time, but I'm trying to stay on top of things.

Over the walls and beyond our main building lie the main halls of Barlinnie. I can hear faint sounds of activity; doors banging and occasional shouting. The thought of that place terrifies me to the bone. Prison makes me afraid but that fear makes me ashamed of myself. I've heard myself scream in the night, a frightened, choked wail; I've denied that it was my voice making the awful sound, in terror, but it was me all right.

The hand will be difficult to carve. I'll have to use my own as a model. Right. Get the tools and the goggles. I look like an explorer in all this gear. The rain's pouring down, which keeps the surface clear but steams up the goggles. This is fine for work. I'll tie my arm with a rope to make the veins more prominent, then copy the rough pattern onto the surface with chalk. The chest is already complete. Now I have to free the arm with only the fingertips touching the chest, near the heart. If I simply rough out the arm from the chest, the stone will be too fragile to polish with the flat chisel, so I have to complete the arm's surface as it emerges: veins first, then bones, then skin. I'll work towards the inside of the arm from both sides.

I'm frozen stiff. My face and hands are numb. I'm soaked through. My legs are aching. Have I pissed myself? I'm so bloody tense: six hours solid. I'll have to eat and come back out tonight, work under the security lights. The arm is just emerging from the stone: the wrist, the knuckles, the veins and the mark of the nail. I wish that I could leave it like that, while it's beautiful, and yet I have to ruin it to prove my technical ability. Well, next I'll do what I want to, make a beautiful sculpture.

Oh, what a wonderful bed, what a wonderful, warm cell. Let's see what's on the news. An armed police officer kills a baby during a house-search; he has been cleared of any criminal charge. The details are irrelevant: the baby is black, the parents are black, they don't matter. Police colleagues are celebrating the decision, in a line outside the court, as though they're at a wedding, toasting the groom; not so much as an apology to the victim's family, no indication of any regret, not a sign of remorse. The police . . .

What? A special meeting? Ajer has called it. Not again!

Around this time the Scottish Office had literally forced a prisoner on the Unit, against the recommendations of the unit psychiatrist, Peter Whitmore. Ian 'Ajer' Adam, a lifer, had a history of mental illness and had been in Broadmoor State Hospital for the Criminally Insane. The Special Unit hadn't been set up to deal with mental illness and had a strict policy concerning prisoners with any psychiatric problems. The community had found from past experience that the pressures of living within such a volatile atmosphere could be disastrous for anyone suffering from any mental disorders. In the early days of the Unit, one case had resulted in violence: a prisoner who had been suffering from extreme paranoia slashed another.

Ajer had become a headache for the authorities. He had been taking prisoners hostage and sexually assaulting them, which didn't cause much concern, but when he began to make threats against staff it was a different matter – no prison would accept him. The Prison Department declared him sane and transferred him to the Special Unit. The prisoners in the Unit normally had a say in such matters to eliminate the possible eruption of vendettas between rivals in the past. Now we were simply told that we would not be charged or transferred in the event of an incident involving Ajer.

He looked fearsome. Derek Marshall, the Principal Officer, had been afraid to open his cell door that first day when he arrived. Fuck! Whit's this guy like?

Within a matter of months it's all beginning to happen. He's doing this deliberately as a wind-up, or he's really beginning to flip his lid. This is the fourth meeting he's called this week alone, all complete nonsense. It's wearing our nerves. Last week I lost count. He's doing people's heads. People are pissed off because you have to go to these meetings even if you have visitors or are doing something more interesting.

The special meetings were created to defuse confrontational or crisis situations, the belief being that through basic discussion problems could be resolved without the usual resort to violence. This helped prisoners to develop skill in debating and had a therapeutic effect in alleviating frustration. Everyone had to attend a special meeting until the matter of concern had been resolved.

Ajer looks disturbed. His eyebrows meet above the bridge of his nose, his middle parting is perfect, not a strand of hair out of place. The hair and moustache are dyed navy-blue. His body hair is like a fur coat. The long arms and sloping forehead lend themselves to comparisons with Neanderthal man. The Missing Link, the Yeti, Bigfoot, Big Stuff: these are a few of the names he's called. He shouldn't be here at all. He's definitely disturbed and needs help.

I don't believe this: a boiled egg? Last week he claimed that one of his budgies had been abducted. Shearer, the Chief, is staring at him: he is just about to finish his shift. People are looking at each other.

'Er, whit time did ye last see the egg, Ajer?'

The staff have to humour him. The prisoners have no qualms about having some fun before their visitors arrive. They're fed up with his antics.

'Ajer, dae ye think this is connected wi' the missing budgie?'

'Eh? Whit dae ye mean?'

He knows he's not being taken seriously, and when he's under pressure he retreats into this repetitive 'Eh? Whit dae ye mean?' only it comes out as one word, and that's all he'll say, 'Ehwhitdaeyemean?'

Ajer called the crisis meeting and he alone can close it: no one can leave the room. Someone suggests that he take all the eggs in the pantry, but he's not having it. He wants the problem resolved properly: that's what the special meetings are for. Shearer asks what he wants from the group.

'Ehwhitdaeyemean?'

Bugsy points out that visitors have been waiting for over an hour.

'Ehwhitdaeyemean?'

My head is bursting. People's tempers are flaring. Ajer says his one word over and over. Shearer can't take any more and orders a transfer.

'Get a cell ready in Barlinnie. I'll call the Prison Department.'

Ajer is totally confused. The meeting has backfired on him.

Bennett and I get him alone.

'Look: call a meeting and apologize, or you're for the cells.'

Shearer can't move him, but Ajer doesn't know that. He calls the meeting and apologizes. Shearer's looking mean, his Fulton McKay face on, right out of *Porridge*, but it works.

'Ajer, these meetings are for crisis situations, not boiled eggs. This behaviour's not on. Now, is that clear?'

'Ehwhitdaeyemean?

I'm so tired of this; tired of the people, tired of the place. I've had seven years of lunatics. We're all mad to be here; only headcases would live this way. How do people here see me? How does the community perceive my behaviour? Surely I'm not the only normal person in the place? That's what we each like to think – but what's my madness?

● Six o'clock. God, I'm tired, I'll have to do more stretching this morning. My gear is still bloody damp. I wonder how the arm looks? I forgot to look at it again last night. Ajer's days are definitely numbered. What's keeping the screws? I want out to work. They should just give us keys instead of all this nonsense of waiting to be let out. I'd be better off in bed. No, I'll finish that arm today and move on to the ribs. Click! Here we go.

'Mornin', Bugsy.'

Jesus it's cold. I love the cold when I'm warm. I'll push myself today, get it done. Shit! I've a visit tonight: that Christian guy's coming to see me. What the hell does he want from me? To draw me back into the fold? I like the Christians I've met, but all this talk about having a personal relationship with Jesus – what a thing to say. They believe Satan is real, too. I can just imagine saying to the Unit psychiatrist, 'Yes, it's true, sir. Jesus talks to me. We have a relationship!'

'Mornin', Hughie.'

Shearer's looking refreshed. 'Ajer okay?'

'He'll pull through. Just chancing his arm.'

Shearer agrees. 'Well, you're nearly finished now, eh? Keep taking the tablets, son.'

The arm's looking good. I'll cut through now and make the gap, free the arm completely. Nice and easy, that's it. I'll do some heavy work to ease the tension. I don't have to think or concentrate, just batter away all day until I'm exhausted. The best part is the nice warm shower afterwards. It's relaxing but I still don't sleep.

Heroin helps me to sleep. Heroin helps with everything: talking to people, facing the lifer, facing the future, facing the mirror. Maybe not: maybe the very opposite – that may be the truth of the heroin. People disapprove, accuse me of abusing my opportunity. Well, I take heroin for pure pleasure, and that's my decision.

Jim, the Christian, likes the statue. 'Christ and the Sinner' – the title emerged in the press. The figure of the Sinner had a technical purpose, to support the weight of the Christ figure. Jim feels that the Sinner is self-explanatory, symbolic. But I no longer look on myself as a sinner: it's too simplistic, Good versus Evil. Jim looks like a social worker with his corduroy jacket, canvas trousers, sensible shoes; his brown hair could be a woolly hat. He goes to great lengths to explain the concept of sin, though he can't define it satisfactorily. Jesus loves him because he is a sinner, yes, he too is a sinner. The heroin makes me euphoric, but I'm extremely interested: I feel comfortable with this. All the religions I've looked at seem to spring from fear of death, the fear of Hell or nothingness. I'm always curious about these things because I'm scared myself. When I ask Jim about belief he becomes quite agitated, appeals to me to have faith. I wish I could believe – in forgiveness, in salvation, in Heaven. He's looking at the ceiling, hands raised, palms upwards. He wants to kneel down and pray with me. I don't see the logic of kneeling down or looking up. These things always throw me: lighting candles, kissing a cross – it's all abracadabra.

Jim's becoming embarrassingly hysterical, freaking out. His eyes are bulging. 'There's a presence here!'

I was just enjoying a conversation and suddenly there's all this. A cup of tea helps to calm him, but he's still convinced there's an evil force present. Jesus, no wonder I take heroin.

I try to humour him. 'Well, after all, this is the Special Unit. Things do get a bit tense, if you know what I mean . . .'

Maybe it's the evil force below. Wullie the Thug? Prisoners are standing round the yard with their visitors, eyeing each other up, whispering snide remarks. The Thug's done up like a headcase as usual, jeans and a skin-tight T-shirt, muscles bulging everywhere. It's the middle of winter, but thugs don't feel the cold. He killed a prisoner in Peterhead, serving fifteen, now plus twenty, years. A real dirty slag. Jim's much more rational now that he's leaving. He has noticed the rippling biceps.

'Who's that, Hugh?'

'Oh, that's our Wullie, a nice guy. Doesn't have many visitors. A shame, eh?'

Jim's eyes are shining. I'm tempted to introduce them: Good meets Evil.

'Well, Jim, goodnight. Aye, it wis nice meeting you too. Drop in again. 'Bye!'

Bobby Brodie's in hysterics when I tell him – he's clocked the Thug too. We can't stop laughing.

'Did ye see him? Ah don't feel pain!'

The Thug hears the laughing upstairs and the paranoia rips out of him. He starts singing to himself. This is the 'I'm-normal' behaviour, nothing-bothers-me behaviour. He's banging the punch-bag now.

'I'm off, Bob, before there's a meeting. See you in the mornin'. Ah don't feel pain.'

Bang! Bang! Bang!

God, what a fucking day!

CHAPTER NINETEEN

BANG! BANG! BANG! The sound of the punch-bag reverberates throughout the cell area. *Bang! Bang! Bang!* The leather gloves are torn to shreds, blood and sweat are squelching between my fingers; sweat is dripping off me. *Bang! Bang!* One, Two. *Bang! Bang! Bang!* One. Two. Three. *Bang! Bang! Bang!* People think I'm depressed. Training all day yesterday, all day today, saying nothing, staying behind my door all night. I'm burning out but I'll keep going till I drop. *Bang! Bang! Bang!* I feel smack running down my throat: I haven't touched it today but I can taste it. My sweat stinks of some sort of chemical, and I can smell it in my cell, too – probably the shit it's cut with, the bastards. I can't get the fucking stuff out of my mind. *Bang! Bang! Bang!* Oh, fuck, I'm feeling sick again, fucking bile coming down my nose. It's not even vomit, just gagging, I'd better get up the stairs before anybody sees me. I hope the phone doesn't go for me.

Jesus! The hairs over my whole body are standing on end. What the fuck's happening? I'll lock the door for the night and tell them I've got the flu if they open me up. Jesus, look at me – look at my eyes. Please stop! Please stop these spasms. I'm jerking all over the place like a fucking dead fish. When the fuck does this stop? I'm boiling and shivering at the same time, sweat's dripping off me. Oh, please, God! Please. Please. Please stop this! My body is screaming for the stuff: please, please help me! I know I've been bad, but I promise, I swear, I'll never ever do anything again. Oh, fuck, I've shit myself – the piss and shit's running out of me. Oh, somebody help me. My head's buried between my knees and I can't control the sobbing. Oh, God. There's one line, the emergency stash. Fuck, I can't get my breath – panting for air – my heartbeat's fluttering. I need that fucking line, just to pull through ... I'll be better prepared, I'll start tomorrow: just one line. I'm screaming for it: just one wee line, that can't set me back. I know I can do it now: cut the dosage down and I'll be okay. The powder's there on the table. I roll a fiver to snort it but I can't. I can't go through this all over again. This is a fucking nightmare. I feel a surge of rage. The powder's scattered on the carpet. What have I done? Oh, fuck, no! I'm snorting fluff, crumbs, dirt, but no fucking powder. I'm shivering and gagging, my skin's crawling. I'm stinking.

I'm praying now, praying aloud. Dear Holy Father, hallowed be Thy name. Thy kingdom come. Thy will be done ... Oh, fuck, help me! Please help me. My fists are banging the carpeted floor. Please, please! You fucking, rotten bastard, I fucking hate you! The Catholic in me rises. Please, I'm sorry, God, I didn't mean that. Honest, I'm sorry. I say another prayer: Hail Mary, full of grace ... I'm drifting into drowsiness, in and out, shivering, jerking, sweating, but no sleeping. I'm exhausted, aching, but can't sleep all night. I just crouch there in a tight ball, my head buried between my knees, all day and all night.

Six o'clock. The door's opened. I don't want to move. My body is aching, my nose is running, my face feels puffy and swollen. The cramps have stopped, but I feel battered and shaken, like in a heavy hangover. I'd still do a line of heroin: I know I want one, even now. The desire is still strong but I'll get through the day without coming apart. I feel dizzy when I stand up, nauseous but not gagging. No taste of smack in my throat. I'll have to shower and clean everything: what a mess. Jesus, the water's like hot needles, my skin aches. I can't get dried properly for the hot flushes and sweating. The sweat's pouring out; still, I'm not jerking all over the place, thank God.

The yard's quiet and dark. The cold air feels crisp. I'm tired but I'll run, pace myself very slowly. I'll just plod on through the day and maybe I'll have some sleep tonight. God, how I long for that, just to sleep without nightmares. I'll keep pushing myself all day. Smack. What a fucking mess.

● *Bang! Bang! Bang!* My hands are swollen and bruised with scabs. I'll have to take it lightly to get going properly. Thank fuck I'm physically fit, otherwise I'd never have pulled through these past three days. *Bang! Bang!* One. Two. *Bang! Bang! Bang!* One. Two. Three. Wish I knew how long this lasts. I can't ask anybody or they'll tipple. *Bang!* One. *Bang! Bang!* One. Two. That's it: get a good rhythm going. *Bang! Bang! Bang!* Thank God the punch-bag doesn't hit back.

Bob's in the yard. 'You okay, Shug?' He knows the score and tells me to get downers to get some sleep.

'Naw, Bob, I'll be brand-new. I'm just a bit fucked.'

Bob's girlfriend arrives and they ask me to have lunch with them.

'Thanks, Bob, but I'm too shattered.'

'Okay, see ye later, wee man.'

Nobody knows, that's good. Bob said they think I'm just pissed off. I'll be left on my own a few days yet, then they'll fire someone in to see how I am. They're decent guys, the screws here; they've lost direction but they're still okay. I'll have to get out of here soon, though; I've been finding the place too difficult. The Thug's fucked the place up with his jail tactics. Jimmy's book didn't help matters either, played right into their hands in the end. I'm supposed to defend the place on my own? I'm sick of the whole fucking lot of them; Jimmy, Ken, Kay, my ma. Fuck them.

● After Jimmy Boyle's transfer the place deteriorated. People think I should keep things going but they just don't realize how much of a vacuum he has left. Jimmy had Ken, Malky and the staff to support his efforts. That's all changed now. No one is interested.

● The rain's cold and I'm still sweating. I love doing this, just walking up and down on my own. Other people are a nightmare. This place forces them on you, talking, day in day out. I'm lucky I can hide in the stone-carving, just give people the body-swerve. This fucking smack. Everything I think about comes right round to it again; it's on my mind always. I'll have to watch all the time: being on a high seems to be my weak point, that's when I hit the drugs, think I'm Jack the fucking Lad. Depression seems to drive the process: I'll fall into a hole and go through the worst and then come out of it on a high. What's the matter with me? That fucking stuff – there are whole families on it, three generations doing it. There's just no stress when you're full of it; you love everybody, everybody's your pal. No wonder people catch it badly; nothing touches you, there's just a glow.

My legs are wobbly. Think I'll have a bath and hit the bunker for the night. I'll block the window with towels to keep the heat in. There's hardly room to get your gear off in here – Malky found the space and squeezed in the bath. It's great for a good long soak after work. Oh, mammy, daddy! Jesus, this is what you call a hot bath! Oh, God, this is wonderful, I could lie here for ever. I love this: lying in darkness in hot water. I feel the tension leaving, heat seeping through me, floating in the warmth. I begin with my toes and work my way up the body to the scalp, tensing then relaxing each muscle. Gradually I'm afloat, watching thoughts drift into focus and then disappear in an instant: millions of them flashing past, some commanding attention for a moment, my reminders to do something. God, I feel so heavy. My body weighs a ton. I can hardly stand up. Jesus, I'm fainting, falling over. Clatter! Bang! I hear the noise of my body hitting the door. I'm panting as I pass out . . .

The doctors ask how I feel. I'm in my own cell, lying on the floor. Malky's smiling at me: 'How do you feel?' I'm wired up to a cardiograph machine, shivering with cold but feeling okay. The doctor's looking into my eyes: fuck, he knows. He's telling them that I'm suffering from exhaustion, that I need lots of rest, and he leaves Valium tablets. The doctor's been a supporter of the Unit for years, a sympathetic sort of guy. I feel much better having fainted, somehow; they thought I'd had a heart attack but it was just the heat – respiratory problems, the doctor says.

Malky's staying behind, making a coffee, blethering away. 'So? What are ye on then?'

There's no point in lying to him. 'Smack. I've been doing it for about eighteen months now.'

The Unit means something to Malky. He believes that it works, though not in the conventional sense. 'Smack? What's it like?' He genuinely wants to know. We talk about it for a while, about the high and low effects. He's interested in the physical signs, no doubt to find out what to watch for in a junkie's behaviour. Smack's the new phenomenon. 'How're ye gonnae deal wi' it then?'

I'm not sure how I'm going to deal with it, to be honest. For the moment I'm through with it, but I just don't know.

Malky suggests that I'm already dealing with it by talking about things. 'Whit ye need is a challenge. Jimmy wis the same, had to be doin' somethin'.'

Jimmy did have to be doing something. He was always working on sculpture or writing his book. *A Sense of Freedom*, his first book, was published while he was still in the Unit and had caused quite a sensation at the time, but he waited until he was released before publishing his second, *The Pain of Confinement*.

*

● I'm past the first stage, but for how long I don't know. I like heroin, I like it a lot, and when I'm through this I'll forget the pain, I'll think I can do it again, just like that. That's the real danger. The good parts outweigh the bad parts. Everything's a bit like that, a bit fucking stupid: monkeys learn quicker.

CHAPTER TWENTY

THE YEARS IN THE Special Unit had been the best years of my life. There's an irony. But things had begun to fracture.

The Scottish Office had deliberately broken the staff continuity. Ken Murray had been transferred, against his will, followed by almost all of the original members of staff. Governor Thomson effectively undermined the cohesion of the group, and new members simply obeyed his orders. Jimmy had recognized what was happening, but he had been given a release date and was moving on to continue a programme at Saughton Prison. (No one was released directly from the Special Unit.) The Prison Department finally tipped the balance by transferring too many prisoners to the Unit within months of each other. They couldn't absorb the philosophy of the place and the situation began to disintegrate into a stand-off between us and them.

The first of the new transfers was Wullie Bennett, serving a life sentence for the murder of another prisoner, with a recommendation for twenty years minimum. Jimmy Boyle had had a long-standing vendetta with him in other prisons; Bennett had vowed to kill him but had reconsidered his intent. In a letter to the Governor he stated that he wanted a chance to rebuild his life and that he could live side by side with Boyle. The letter had been written from the Inverness cages.

Bennett's reputation preceded him: he'd been the subject of an investigation into prison rape involving forty cases in Aberdeen Prison. Everyone was alarmed. Bennett's transfer posed several problems, including that of his influence over other prisoners; and I had my own fears. What if I became so fearful that I stabbed him? Who was going to confront the guy?

Jimmy tried to reassure me. 'Look, he's a bampot, but a dangerous bampot. The way to beat him is to outfox him. The way to outfox him is to rely on the meetings. He'll play on jail culture, but the meetings are yer only strength – that's the way to deal with him.'

When Jimmy left I felt a terrible sense of loss. He had given me his stone-carving tools, a load of old tenement blocks and a small, tattered jungle hat. I'd even moved into his work space, but there was no substitute for his company and his insight.

Bennett looked physically slight, but when he stripped off he had muscles on top of muscles. He had a powerful presence. When Jimmy left there had been a special meeting afterwards, and someone had asked about the contents of Jimmy's diaries, while someone else had mentioned suing him. It was obvious what was going on, and Bennett had picked it up at once. He launched into an attack on the art work.

'Aye, all that art crap as well. A load a fuckin' shite.'

I turned to him. 'Jimmy's away now. This you flexin' yer muscles already? Why did ye wait till he left?' I was afraid but I had to make my position clear. 'I'll be doin' art work whether ye like it or not. Ye don't fuckin' decide how I run my life, okay?'

He was just sitting there, considering me. Later that night I went down to his cell, with two knives up my sleeve. He was from another generation, older than me and more cunning.

'Look,' I said, 'I hope ye don't think I wis hidin' behind the screws this afternoon. I'll perform wi' you wherever ye like.'

'Ye're gettin' a bit heavy,' he said.

'I'll go as heavy as ye want.'

'You deal wi' your division up the stairs, an Ah'll deal wi' the bottom flat. Fair enough?'

He was declaring a division of territory: that was how he saw the place. Bobby Brodie laughed when I told him what had happened but agreed that Bennett was a threat to the place. He reckoned that he was obsessed with Boyle and would try to destroy the Unit because of that.

Bennett began to influence the staff. His black humour appealed to them. They had become more comfortable listening to his jokes than discussing the problems facing the Unit. They were having an easy time now, paying lip-service to the meetings. It was a good number.

● At Christmas people always made an effort to let bygones be bygones. We celebrated as a group, having a drink with the staff and later among ourselves. That Christmas Bobby and I were invited down to Ajer's cell. Bennett and Steen were there already, rolling some joints.

There's tension but the patter's rolling a hundred miles an hour, joke after joke; everyone's stoned. Someone's talking seriously about Ajer's girlfriend, Evie, who has to be escorted by a social worker when she comes to visit.

'Ajer, ye want tae get rid of that Evie. She's an embarrassment to the whole fuckin' place.'

'Naw, Ah cannae dae that. Evie gave me a wee spell.'

A wee spell? You never ask anyone what they're in for but, being stoned, I stumble in with the awkward question. 'A wee spell? Whit's he on aboot?'

Everyone's giggling. I've bloomered but it's too late. Steen says, 'Tell Collie whit yer in for.'

The minute he says it, they're all in.

'Aye, tell him. Tell him aboot the dwarf, the wee midget.'

There had been a midget staying at their flat in Partick. Ajer suspected he'd been having it off with Evie. One day he came back to the flat early and hid himself under the bed; sure enough, in jumps the midget with his Evie.

Ajer grabbed him by the ankles and swung him round the room, battering his head to a pulp. Having killed him, he then carved up the body and hid parts all over the flat. The torso he put up the chimney, the head in a cupboard. The place was stinking.

'How did ye get found out?' (I'm turning white by now as Ajer matter-of-factly explains what happened.)

'Well, I'd stolen a TV set, and the coppers came up tae turn me o'er. When they opened the back tae check the serial number, they found an arm inside, holdin' some intestines. One daft copper fainted, but they found the rest o' the body in cupboards an' drawers.'

I'm almost ill but keep on with the obvious. 'Whit's that got tae dae wi' a wee spell, though?'

'Well, Collie. Ah'd just done the head, the torso an' arms. Ah wis knackered – dae ye know whit Ah mean? Anyway, Evie came in an' said. "Ajer, go an' have yer tea, an' Ah'll gie ye a wee spell."'

The place erupted. Everyone's in hysterics, hearing the story. Ajer's just staring into space, no doubt reminiscing, but I can't believe it. A wee fucking spell? The guy had to be kidding – but he wasn't, that was the scary part; he was deadly serious, attached to her because of her concern for his tiredness.

• Bobby Brodie and I discussed the story a few days later. There were six guys in the Unit, all trying to act normal: Ajer walking round at six in the morning in a three-piece suit; Bennett pretending that he didn't feel any physical pain, being macho; Steen posing for photographs with two toy shotguns; Mac-Pherson here for protection . . .

'Bobby, I'm on the first fuckin' bus out of here! Are we off our heads as well, or are we the only two normal people in the fuckin' place?'

Bill MacPherson had been transferred within months of Ajer. He was serving twenty-six years for bank robbery, with an additional six for his part in the riot with Jimmy Boyle at the Inverness cages. He'd been stabbed, almost killed, by a prisoner from London in Peterhead, and while he was in the segregated hospital wing, prisoners had made another attempt on his life.

Bill was the opposite of Ajer, a highly articulate man with radical socialist leanings. People found him very difficult to confront in the meetings; his sharp wit and intelligence had no match in debates, and he tore people's arguments to ribbons. He had become very bitter; although he was intelligent, he wasn't cunning. Bennett knew how to exploit him, turning him into a verbal rocket against me.

(The meetings were opportunities to let off steam, and at the beginning I had really gone for people, too, but Jimmy had tried to put me right. 'Just make your points,' he said. 'Don't stamp people into the ground and destroy them. They've got to live with themselves.')

The Scottish Office then replaced Governor Thomson with Bill Davidson, from Aberdeen. Davidson had worked his way up through the ranks and was steeped in jail culture. He'd been at Aberdeen with Bennett, and his attitude was that, as Wullie had never assaulted staff, he was a decent enough prisoner.

At this point prisoners were reluctant to call meetings for fear of being regarded as grasses – unless they were to complain about Bobby Brodie or me. The management and staff allowed the rot to set in, despite our efforts to maintain the group meetings. Bennett had prostitutes and young boys visiting him, but even when that was raised in a meeting no one said a word. Plenty was said about the Christ statue, however. The church which had commissioned it had rejected the finished work on the grounds of obscenity, and I had to face the community every day to account for the controversy whipped up by the tabloid press and to determine when it would be removed from the Unit.

The place had become a madhouse, as far as I was concerned.

Prisoners were now competing with each other on every level. I bought a colour television. Bennett bought a bigger one. He bought a stereo unit. I bought a bigger one. You couldn't leave your cell without attention to your appearance, otherwise there'd be snide comments: 'Did ye see the state he's in? I threw out the same kind of sweatshirt last week . . .'

It all seemed orderly on the surface, with everyone walking round smartly dressed, but the reality was total disorder.

Bennett had found his way into the heroin scene on the outside, and dealers began to visit on a regular basis, dressed in all the usual rubbish – gold chains and rings. In Possilpark a young boy died from an overdose of uncut heroin, and the press said it had come from Bennett. I expected a special meeting to be called, but there was not a word. I felt frustrated that I'd no opportunity to expose him even in the recorded minutes of a meeting. I'd buried my nose in the very same powder: who was I to criticize Bennett?

● One night Bugsy brought in a video on his night-shift duty. It was Jimmy's film, *A Sense of Freedom*. As we watched it, I thought I heard someone shouting from his window, which was unusual. Nobody in the Unit ever shouted from his window at night, unlike the mainstream prisons. I was about to settle down after the film when I heard it again, this time much clearer. It was Bennett.

'Collie's a poof!'

That's nice, coming from him, I thought. He sounded high, almost incoherent. Bugsy tried to quieten him down, but I knew we were going to be entertained. When he had finished mouthing off at me, he went round each of the prisoners in turn. He was very funny – I could hear the other guy laughing too. The final touch was his selection of music.

'Here! Dae yes want tae hear some music, eh? Here's a right bitta culture for ye. Wait til yes hear Wullie's Desert Island Discs! Mantovani!'

You could hear it all over Riddrie.

'Sense o' freedom, eh? Ya fuckin' bampots.'

The next morning we had a meeting. Bennett sat with his head bowed and I loved every minute of it. Total humiliation. He said that he'd been under pressure because his mother was ill and apologized for his behaviour.

The Governor raised his hands. 'Wullie! Why didn't ye tell somebody? We'd have tried to help.'

But nobody was confronting Bennett directly. I proposed that his visits be supervised until he revealed who brought in the drink, and gradually people put up their hands to vote that his visits be sanctioned. It had to be a major breakthrough for the group as a whole. His hold had finally been broken through his own stupidity; things could improve now.

When I returned to the cell area, Bennett was there, glaring at everyone. 'When that gate's locked, Ah'm goin roon every wan ey ye's. Ah'm gonnae break yer fuckin jaws.'

'Yer no breakin' ma fuckin' jaw!'

We stood facing each other, staring for a few seconds. I turned away and *bang!* I hit the wall behind from the impact, but used it for leverage. I rammed the nut on him from the ankles upwards, full force, and he fell flat on his back. Before I could move, the screws were on me. They had no idea what had happened. There was total panic.

The chief confronted us both at the meeting a few minutes later. 'Right. Whit happened?'

'Ah fell, that's all. Nothin' happened,' said Bennett.

Shearer, Bennett and I remained in the room after everyone left. Shearer spoke first. 'Right, you two, this can't go on. The fuckin' place is a shambles with all this carry-on. Boyle's fuckin' out, so whit's the problem wi' you?'

Bennett admitted that his head had been done in by reading Jimmy's second book, *The Pain of Confinement*. 'Ah gave my fuckin' word comin' here, an' then he slags me again. Ma two boys have tae live wi' that fuckin' shite he wrote aboot me.'

I pointed out that this shouldn't have affected the Unit, but we agreed on a fresh start and the air was cleared. Things began to improve. The meetings edged back towards being constructive.

Malky was genuinely concerned about Bennett. 'Look,' he said, 'he knows what he is. And as far as Ah'm concerned, that's the first step. We're not looking for angels in here. You and Jimmy – he's not got yer brains. Allow him tae develop tae some level that's acceptable tae him and tae the people outside. That's what it's all aboot.'

● I still had to deal with the statue of Christ. I had been approached by an agent, Jim Duffy, who said he was acting on behalf of a party in America who wished to remain anonymous. I didn't know how much to ask for the work and consulted Kay Carmichael and Donald McDonald, the minister who had commissioned it.

Kay was concerned. 'Hugh, this could be the mafia. They could be using it to smuggle drugs.'

'Kay,' I said, embarrassed, 'I'm in the jail. I'm in Barlinnie. The fuckin' mafia's never heard of Glasgow, never mind the Unit. Get a grip!'

Donald McDonald, though he also had his doubts, said that he wouldn't value the statue at less than £8,000. Jim Duffy agreed and arranged to meet me at the Glasgow School of Art on my next day out. I'd been going there once a week, and, though it was closed for the summer holidays, we'd have lunch at the Third Eye centre nearby at twelve o'clock.

Governor Davidson had said there'd be no problem. I could go out as normal but shouldn't stray beyond Sauchiehall Street.

Jim Duffy failed to make the meeting. At precisely twelve noon there was an anonymous phone call to the Special Unit, stating that Hugh Collins was at Central Station carrying a suitcase with £10,000 in it, a gun and a ticket to London.

I went along to Nico's in Sauchiehall Street, where the art

students often went, and had a bar lunch. Out of the corner of my eye I saw a picture of myself flash up on the television behind the bar. Probably something to do with the Christ statue. After a while, a few heads turned in my direction – the scar along my jaw is conspicuous – but it wasn't until some students arrived that I realized something was wrong.

'Hugh! The police are looking for you everywhere. They're telling people not to approach you, that you could be armed and dangerous.'

What the fuck was going on? I couldn't fathom what was happening. I rang my mother.

'Hughie! Whatever are ye daein', son? Get gack tae the Unit as fast as possible. Get a taxi right now. They've been here lookin' for ye, so don't waste time, jist get back tae the jail.'

For a brief moment I thought of getting myself a gun, just in case, but I pulled myself together and jumped in a taxi. 'Take me tae Barlinnie. Fast as ye can, pal.'

A crowd of journalists had gathered outside the prison, and I still had no idea what was going on. I managed to get inside before they reached me but hadn't expected to be met by a reception party in riot gear.

'Right, Collins, put down the weapons. Put down the toolbag.'

I began to worry when I found myself in the strong cell of the mainstream part of the prison.

Apparently, Governor Davidson had taken the anonymous phone call about me being on the run. He had then immediately contacted the Prison Department rather than waiting to see if there was any truth behind the call. I mean, I had no reason to go on the trot, and why all this stuff about the gun and London?

Anyone with an ounce of common sense would have realized the call was a hoax or that this was all some sort of set-up. I don't believe the Governor was that stupid. I think he had a fair idea of what would happen when news was leaked that one of the Special Unit prisoners was loose on the streets with a gun.

The Prison Department notified the police and, as one would expect, a nationwide police manhunt was launched. There I was, all the time, totally unaware of the fuss, having a coffee in Nico's Bar in Sauchiehall Street. The Scottish Information Office then leaked the news to the press: I hit the headlines and for a few weeks the press had a field day, running all the usual stories about security at the jail, all the usual indignation about prisoners' release programmes endangering the public.

While I lay in the cells, the Governor wasn't having an easy time. He found himself in the centre of a controversy. This wasn't going to blow over without a stink – there were a lot of questions being asked, concerning who had let me out? Or had I just walked out on my own? Who had signed the release licence? Someone had to know the school was closed. Who was responsible? Who fucked up?

The incident had become an embarrassment to the authorities, partly due to the fact that I had returned to the prison immediately on hearing of my own escape. There were what seemed to be wee flaws in the Governor's account on the matter – wee fibs, tiny white lies.

Tony Jones, the director of Glasgow Art School, informed the press that the prison had known that the school would be on holiday. He said that he had called the prison himself for clarification on arrangements.

Governor Davidson denied that he had known that the school was on holiday; he denied that he'd signed my release licence. He then stated that a prisoner had taken the call from the Art School. Yes, you could say his head was on the chopping-block.

When he discovered that I had returned to the prison, he immediately called a meeting to inform the community of the situation. The policy on transfers to date had been that any prisoner about to be moved was given the opportunity to explain his actions before the community – but not so in my case.

Davidson called the meeting but basically to blackmail it into voting me out without any opportunity for me to explain what had happened. 'If Collins is voted back in, then I'm walking out of here.' You can't afford to lose another governor in any circumstances.

Governors in the past had rarely lasted long in the Unit, so he had them by the balls. The problem had been the Governors' position within the community: they had to account for every decision taken which undermined their power base. This had caused many to leave and also a number of nervous breakdowns in the process, particularly for those who had tried to deny the power of community politics. Davidson was fighting to hang onto his career. He forced my transfer through.

He then breached prison procedure by having my cell searched in my absence. Prisoners must be present during a search, but he ransacked my cell and found my personal diary: 'Collins, I think this breaches prison security,' he said. 'These diaries will be confiscated under the Official Secrets Act. Oh, and by the way, ye're bein' transferred up the road. Ye're goin' tae Peterhead.'

I felt like punching the sneer off his fat face, but I had to keep things together. Peter-fuckin'-head! Is that fuckin' right? Dae they hiv tiger's up there or something'? I spat back at him, trying to hang onto some bravado. The Scottish Office then formally informed me that I was to be transferred there, just as that wanker had said. Peterhead? There are fucking riots going on up there just now. Fuck this, I thought. I declared that I was on a hunger strike: this would delay the transfer and give my ma time to work something out.

Thankfully, Bugsy Moran contacted my ma. Bugsy had been present during the meeting when the Governor had been informed of the art-school holiday period and the decision to let me go out regardless. Indeed, Bugsy had a copy of the minutes of the meeting, which he wanted my ma to have as a lever against the authorities. 'Betty,' he said, 'Hughie was set up and everybody knows that, but naebidy really has the bottle tae go up against Davidson.'

My ma contacted the Scottish Office: 'Ma son better get a fair deal or this lot finds its way intae the press,' she told them.

Bugsy came to see me afterwards in the cells to let me know what was happening. 'Davidson's shittin' 'imsel'.' He laughed. 'He's panickin'. He even asked me tae talk tae yer ma. He wants tae find oot who the mole is.' Bugsy was in hysterics laughing. 'Fuck! If they find out it's me they'll fucking sack me! The mole, eh, for fuck's sake!'

Davidson later came to my cell, a trifle subdued. 'Hughie . . . eh . . . Yer ma's . . . eh . . . she's gonnae get me the sack, son. God, I've got a family. Please, kin ye no talk tae her?'

I cut him dead. I'm lying there on the floor. I have filthy blankets over me, and I'm starving myself. Oh, it's Hughie now is it? Listen, I want Saughton! I want my tools, right? My ma will blow you apart, so I want a progressive transfer and my name cleared with the Prison Department. You fucked up, so don't use me to save your fuckin' career, 'cos I've done fuck-all to deserve this, you bastard.

Davidson was on his knees, pleading with me. 'Ah promise that I'll get ye the best deal but talk tae yer ma, please! That mob o'er there voted ye oot, Hughie. Honest! They voted against ye, it was nothin' tae dae wi' me.'

The Scottish Office had to relent in the end. My ma forced them to give me a fair deal, but they weren't happy about the transfer. They warned me to be careful. 'Lift your hands to anybody and you will never see daylight, Collins.'

The Special Unit had become a political embarrassment over the years. For the main part, the Unit worked but what the prison authorities hated was that they had been proved wrong on the question of treatment. Prisoners like myself had shown that we were not animals: we had shown that if we were treated properly, then we in turn could respond, possibly even change. But what they despised most was the success of one man, Jimmy Boyle.

Well, Saughton Prison it was. Edinburgh wasn't too far. I wouldn't be completely cut off from friends and family. The prison was fairly quiet compared to other establishments but there would be problems ahead.

CHAPTER TWENTY-ONE

●

SAUGHTON PRISON, 1985.
    Have I changed? I think differently, see things differently, do things differently: is that change? The prison system itself has adopted a new approach, 'Dare to Care' – care for the 'clients', as the prisoners are now regarded, clients who live in rooms as opposed to cells. Staff are now providing a social service, not just counting bodies. So I'm a client now, residing in a room of B/Wing, H M P Saughton, Edinburgh. The business of caring for the offender sounds challenging: staff and clients are on first-name terms. The theme of trust and responsibility sounds familiar: haven't I heard this before somewhere?

Wullie Bennett has put a contract on me. Fats Lovell, one of the clients here, is the rocket: he's going to stab me for a few pills' payment. It's some contract; there must be a discount.

The Tank Commander is telling me all this. He's the Governor of the wing. No, he doesn't know what hall Lovell's in, but staff will be watching, yes, watching me – maybe they think I'm going to stab myself? The Commander tells me, 'You can expect no special treatment here, Collins. This is a prison, not a facility for would-be artists.'

'Dae Ah detect a wee dig there, sir?'

Lovell turns out to be next door to me – what a coincidence! I pull him on the way back from the dining hall: the hall is crowded with guys shouting and slamming doors shut. He's not expecting this. He's stammering that there's been a mistake, pleading that I have got things all wrong about the contract: 'Honest, Shug, Ah'm finished wi' that cunt Bennett.'

'Ah'll put you under a fuckin' bed, Fats. One fuckin' look frae you an' ye're in trouble, okay?'

I know I can't move, but Fats doesn't know that. All he knows is that his bluff has been called in front of his pals: he's just a jail bam, a rocket.

I spend three months watching my back: the place is heaving with drugs and the junkies would stab anyone for a hit. I don't like what I'm doing but I've no choice: discussion groups don't exist in jail. Violence or the threat of it is the language here. You don't say, 'Let's have a chat, pal.'

I'm moved to C Hall and my new room-mate is Pie, named for the way his face is shaped. Pie has been told by the staff that I'm a child-molester, a child-killer. He's waiting for me, standing in the middle of the room with clenched fists and clenched jaw.

'Ah heard you're a fuckin' beast.'

The pisspot on the bed indicates where I'm to sleep; the pin-ups of the Queen covering the wall tell me that he's a Protestant; the pipe-band flute on the table confirms that he's a religious bigot, an Orangeman. The Glasgow accent is put on, to make him sound hard.

'Ah'm in fur attempt murder, ye know.'

The truth is that he's from a small village in the hills, has never been in prison before and is serving six months as a first offender.

Pie's whole demeanour changes after tea: someone has told him that I'm from the Special Unit and that I'm a friend of Jimmy Boyle. Jesus! Pie has bloomered drastically.

'Shug, look. They fuckin' screws told me you were a beast.

Honest, I'll fuckin' kill the bastards!' He's punching the cell door for effect. 'Fuckin' bastards, Shug!'

Pie and I spend most of those six months together. He can't read or write but he can talk, non-stop chatter. He drives me mad with questions. 'Here, Shug! Whit's that Boyle like?' 'Here, Shug! Whit's that Unit like?' Whenever I pick up a book, he starts. 'Here, Shug! Whit's the book like?'

He doesn't read at all, as I say, not even his mail. He keeps the perfumed letters, the others he dumps in the bin. He simply sniffs the mail at night, staring into space, thinking of his wife at home, of his family, remembering. I write letters to his wife for him. Sometimes I write the most romantic nonsense – that he's fallen in love with an officer, for example. She thinks he's gone mad. I torture him by telling lies: that she's leaving him for another man, that the perfume is really after-shave. I wait until he's almost in tears before telling the truth: 'Only kiddin'. Pie!' I love tormenting him because he drives me crazy: it's my revenge. He plays the flute while I'm trying to read; he shadow-boxes while I'm trying to read; he pisses and farts while I'm trying to read. And all the time he's asking questions. 'Ever saw one this size, eh, Shug?' Yes, I love tormenting him every chance I get, every moment.

I watch him falling asleep: he's out tomorrow, thank God. I tie his hands and feet together with socks, he's trussed up like a chicken. I throw a basin of cold water over him.

'Ya bastard, Shug!' He knows he's in for the treatment and begs me to untie him. 'Shug, please! The doors are open soon! C'mon, ya bastard!'

Six thirty: the cell fills with prisoners. I leave for the gymnasium. Pie's screaming and there are shrieks of laughter. When I come back I can't stop laughing: Pie's covered in boot polish, his eyebrows are gone, his false teeth are missing and he's still tied up. 'You! Ya dirty bastard!'

He's being tough again later in the morning. He doesn't want to leave me behind because I'm his best mate, his pal, his china.

I'll miss him – he's been entertaining, he claims. Prison has too many men like me, cardboard gangsters, bores, bampots. Pie has been time out, a laugh.

He doesn't want to go, so why not batter a screw? I suggest. Then we'd get another six months together. Aye, let's punch a screw . . .

'Whit? Are ye fuckin' kiddin'? Fuck you! I'll send ye a postcard!'

Well, I haven't been stabbed or stabbed anyone; thankfully Pie didn't go for me as a beast. The screws are disappointed. I don't trust a single one of them. They all try to be macho, talking tough prison jargon, looking hard-eyed. It's quite embarrassing. The younger ones are mostly keep-fit fanatics, training for unarmed combat and bursting with aggression. They've been told that I'm dangerous, a disturbed person, half-mad. I'm pretending that I've changed, behaving to get out on parole. They can't resist talking to me: they don't like me but they can't stay away, wanting to identify with me. The violent image is irresistible, the notoriety is magnetic. Jimmy would have served about a hundred years if all their claims to have worked with him were true; Larry Winters, too: 'Aye, never gave *me* any problems.' Now it's my turn. They want to get the strength of me, control me, but they can't. I'm civil to everyone in prison but don't voluntarily make conversation: when someone speaks to me, they want something from me.

I train in the gymnasium every single morning at six thirty and in the evening at six thirty, doing weights, yoga and sparring in an unvarying routine. This provides a degree of privacy; the consistency gives me a breathing space. I detest physical exertion and am basically lazy, but I'm a man in a man's world. Like them, I pretend to be hard: my disciplined training routine is hard; my deliberate silence is hard; my battered, scarred face is hard. They want to be hard, to be real men, men's men, male. Being male, they have to impress, prove their masculinity, prove that they have power, that they don't feel pain, that they don't have feelings. I'm playing the same game. I'm hard. I have power and no feelings. I'm trying to impress other men. There are no women here: men are impressing men in the male world of the prison. Is this homosexuality? Is it fear? Who knows: this is how males behave in a male environment. I'm playing a macho game on a reputation long past its sell-by date. I'm playing the dangerous man in order to prevent confrontations, to prevent being found out, to prevent being exposed as moody and ordinary. The population believes that I've been put through the grinder, that I've survived terrible beatings. I have, but they don't know the cost. They believe that this makes me the hard man.

Playing this role protects me from harm, provides a safe passage through prison, but it's a stage performance, a live show. The screws have only to call my bluff to find that out, and yet they can't do that without endangering their own lives, obedient to the threat of violence against them. Clients? Prisoners are bodies, mere numbers, nothing more. Screws have tried twice to cause an incident, and if Fats and Pie had been difficult, they could have done me. Fortunately, prisoners think I'm a decent guy: I don't bully, I take a joint at times, I laugh at myself and my situation. I'm just one of the boys. Prisoners are at ease with me, and supportive – after all, I've done screws, so I'm like a hero.

When the screws put on the pressure directly, I deliberately look disturbed. I am dishevelled, unwashed and unshaven, my hair stands on end. A Loony Toon. I distance myself, refusing work routines and recreational facilities, any form of communication. I become hostile when I'm outnumbered, physically threatening – that's an impressive part. Basically I throw a tantrum, and it works! This carefully disarranged look never fails: they back off on sight, leave me alone. What a joke: I'm lying in bed with a book, and they're tiptoeing around, thinking that I'm planning a murder ... I'm not suffering from mental illness. I believe that people decide to be violent, to be out of control, unless they're genuinely insane. At some point there is a decision, when you think, Fuck it, that's it. I want out of prison now, and I see some hope of it, so I have no reason to be violent. What will I do if they call my bluff? I'll make a decision: I will be violent, or I'll laugh at their stupidity. I don't care what they think, nothing else matters to me but my survival.

● I never read political books; I didn't want to become politically aware. Every prison has its political agitators, talking about what will happen when the revolution starts – a load of bollocks. I used books as chewing-gum: cowboy stories, adventures, anything fictional: an escape. Political books would have been too dangerous for me; they'd have provided a reason to be angry, been a cause for violence. I could have blamed what had happened on a system, and on the people who embodied it, and then I could have justified to myself my violent reactions.

In Perth Prison, when I got bored, I'd be swamped in self-pity, really rolling in it. Why me? How had I ended up in solitary? And yet the total isolation did give me a chance to concentrate on what was going on in my own mind. When I did yoga exercises, I'd focus on certain aspects of my life: memories of places, and of people – Eileen, Lynn, my granny – which in many ways was like going home again.

I'd recall all the details of the street where we lived, going into the front close . . . The bottom part of the close wall was painted dark brown and it was always clean because the women leathered you if it wasn't; then there was a thin black line, and above that the wall could be whitewashed over, so the kids scribbled on that part. Climbing the stairs to the door with its huge brass handle. The middle landing had a sash window where I hid my liquorice straps as a kid and my machete blades as a teenager. Our landing was spotless. Going into our lobby: cheap wallpaper with tiny flowers; the toilet on the right with a green door, half glass with a crack in it; then the press where I'd hide the shoplifted toys; then the kitchen, with a dirty old carpet that I used to sweep for hours. Two doors at the end of the lobby into the big bedroom and the living room, always fresh-smelling with the windows open. In Cathie's room, to the left, there was a sickly smell of all sorts of perfumes, and her underwear would be scattered over the bed.

I could visualize all that perfectly, I did it so many times in prison. Once I'd gone over the physical structure, I'd remember a specific incident, recall people's voices, remember how my granny smelled. I think this preserved my sanity. I'd do it for a vacation, and afterwards fall asleep instead of climbing the walls. It certainly helped me to hang on to a reality in my life; drifting into a fantasy world was always a danger in solitary.

I could actually feel the presence of my granny, smell her working apron. She worked during the day as a dish-washer at the Grosvenor Hotel and in the evenings did office-cleaning jobs. She was on her feet all the time, and got corns and hard skin as a result. When she came home, late in the evening, she'd sit by the fire while I washed her feet in a basin of hot water. Then I'd climb on to her huge lap and fall asleep on her enormous breasts, conscious of her breathing and completely secure in her warmth. The shape of her feet is engraved on my mind – I sculpted them in stone for a ballet dancer, in a pirouette.

In Saughton Prison I remember lying on my bed just staring at the light bulb, and suddenly I thought – like in the old cartoon where bulb = bum – that it looked like Auld Cathie. It was one of the memories I had of her: her huge bum, swaying like an elephant's. You know how you see your mother from behind, bending over, maybe washing stairs or something, that big arse swaying. I began to draw that shape in charcoal, drawings twelve to sixteen feet high: huge naked women with big breasts, wide hips and massive, chunky feet, all cradling babies. They brought to the surface all sorts of buried emotions. The feelings I had about my granny, and those feet, they had a kind of solidity, feelings beyond the enduring anger about confinement.

The screws laughed at the drawings but kids visiting liked them: 'Look, there's ma mammy!' I later carved the image of a huge mother and child from a twelve-ton block of granite for a local housing scheme in a deprived area of Edinburgh.

Most days, though, I felt like banging one of the screws on the jaw. I put a distance between us but I couldn't help those feelings. What stopped me was simply the hope of being released. To be released would be to be free from pain: prison is a painful process, lonely and frustrating. Fear and anger lay always just below the surface, powerful feelings that sometimes made me want to kill. My behaviour was determined by fear: the fear of losing hope, the fear of life in prison. Can a different face of fear be defined as change? If so, have I really changed?

I think if I'd been released straight from the Unit, I wouldn't have felt as bitter or had so much rage inside. After eight or ten years I could have been gradually fed back into the world, and if I'd made any bloomers then, they would have been purely in connection with the art world. I took myself far too seriously as an artist and would have had to suffer the indignities of any art student in discovering the realities, but I wouldn't have been a threat to the public. The violent part of my life had ended.

The next eight years really twisted me inside. Although I'd mentally accepted that I would serve fifteen years to appease society's need for revenge, those final years actually put society in danger again, creating a time-bomb just waiting to go off. They ruined all the work that had been done in the Special Unit, where I'd developed into a reasonable sort of person.

The Unit gave people space to think things through – women and relationships and your position in the world. Change is the word that troubles me, I'm reluctant to use it in my case. It conjures up a new identity, something merely adopted, a fictional character. My attitude to women certainly altered in many ways. Once the women in my life had been there to provide sex or carry knives, that sort of thing. Some of my visitors to the Unit challenged that attitude, and for the first time in my life I had friends who were women, people who just happened to be female.

The Unit encouraged communication, people talking, having discussions. This was all new to me. I'd never sat in a group like that before. My only conversations in prison had been with other criminals, talking about who'd been stabbed or who'd robbed what bank. It was another world. When I was arrested I didn't know who was Prime Minister – er, was it Harry Wilson? I didn't even know the Queen's surname – eh, Mrs Tudor?

Despite that life I've led, I've never actually thought of myself as a criminal. I don't believe I think like a criminal, planning things ahead. I was an opportunist, reckless – dangerously reckless. Perhaps that's criminal behaviour, and I'm excusing myself in my interpretation of premeditation.

Albert, I think, was driven by having grown up poor. That didn't bother me. Don't get me wrong. I enjoyed acquiring things – all those suits, the glamour and the women. I was attracted by the power. But when I was younger, I'd have been quite content to have had a family of my own, a real job earning money, a domesticated life. Perhaps I would have got bored or disillusioned, the monster that was there might still have surfaced, but my ambitions were fairly normal as a young boy, nothing unusual or odd.

I dreamed of being a policeman, of joining the army, even of becoming a priest. Auld Cathie, despite her harsh life, was a devout Catholic, and a priest in the family wouldn't have seemed unusual. People need something to believe in – money, career, religion, whatever – and I was no different from anybody else, only with me it was God. The anger in me – and it's still there – is partly because I believed and yet I was allowed to murder someone. God knows and sees everything, doesn't he? Isn't that what we were taught in our Catholic schools? Well, why did he let me kill somebody? Why didn't he prevent it from happening? Why? Because it's all nonsense, that's why. White man's magic, abracadabra.

The last thing I wanted to do was to kill someone. Mulligan and Albert were the same. We carried knives and were reckless. I met a guy the other day, an ex-lifer, and he showed me the knife he was carrying.

'What the fuck are you doin' wi' that thing?' I asked.

'Oh, just in case,' he said.

My belief is that if you're carrying a weapon, it'll be used: a gun, a knife, an iron bar. There've been times since being released when I've thought of acquiring a gun – just in case. But I know that I might get drunk, I might get carried away, I might kill someone in a fight.

I'm not a secure person. If I feel threatened, I overreact. A lot of men do that, men who haven't committed murder, men who put on a macho act, trying to look dangerous. I hate to use the word self-control. That's all it is: mental control. It can snap. I enjoyed being violent. I got a buzz from it. Some people have the same high driving a speedboat, or a fast car, or rock-climbing – the thrill of danger – but with me it's violence. I should have joined the army, and killed people without such costly consequences. It's legal to kill people in the armed forces. Shit, why didn't I just become a paratrooper?

In prison the authorities always say, 'It's a normal world out there. How are you going to fit back into society?' I walked out, and found total chaos. Normal? Really, I don't know what normal is. I try to make a mess in our flat because that's normal, it's a natural order. In prison, everything's perfect, not a thing out of place – or you're punished. Caroline dumps things down in the flat and I catch myself getting annoyed. That's the jail coming out in me, trying to keep it all nice and tidy, all neat and perfect, all under complete control. It's a form of insanity.

In prison I kidded myself on that I had control of the whole jail. I had to run the hall, know everything that was going on, dominate everything – that was my form of security. Actually the prison was controlling me, determining my daily behaviour.

One of my fears was that I'd be lost in the population, a bampot with no identity, just another daft lifer.

I think that same fear drove me to the stone-carving and drawing at first. The same violent energy lent itself to that drive, that need to be somebody, even in jail. Stone-carving is a macho thing, too – you never see female stone-carvers, do you? They've been excluded from that aspect of art. In the Unit I had to learn to deal with that fear, and the stone-carving helped in many ways. It gave me the old sense of power, of being macho and all that. I developed a disciplined routine – exercising, working, communicating, educating myself – but there was a falseness in it. Deep inside I was still like a frightened wee boy in a man's world. I was still angry and confused about the murder, but if I had expressed those feelings too often, the authorities would have said that I was disturbed. I had to demonstrate by my behaviour that I'd come to terms with the murder and could get on with my life in a normal fashion. Yes, sure, it never happened, did it?

The Special Unit was a very fashionable place for the intelligentsia to visit. I felt like a pet lion, except that the leash was getting longer. All I had to do was to polish up my act in terms of speech and manners, be charming at all times and never show my teeth. I became very manipulative and thrived on the intrigues and the internal politics, like a psychological predator. Having discovered big words, I became over-articulate and over-confident; it was embarrassing – verbal diarrhoea. When Jimmy left I stamped my personality all over the Unit by displaying drawings and sculptures, talking to visitors, talking to staff. I mean, I was the artist now, wasn't I? The reformed killer and all that?

The Christ statue? Well, I poured the horrors of my guilt into that, but that doesn't make it art. It was saturated with my personality; it's my guilt crystallized in stone, in a solid, visual form. I hate the sight of the statue, but it did allow me to move on to works that didn't have me stamped all over them. I see art as motion. The personality is transitory experiences, a form of language. Hugh Collins is accumulated experience, psychological dross. Art, like life, is ongoing, eternal and abstract. It has its own beauty. The motion in itself is beauty, not the end product.

Saughton fucked me around with my tools, my work and a release programme. Possibly if they had fulfilled the promises made to me, I would have emerged as a less dangerous person. I don't know; maybe it wasn't just that. It was the focus on me, and all the strokes they tried to pull. I'd go through all the proper channels, trying to play the game with them, and they would fuck me over time after time.

With the tools it was a screw they called Cockroach. He boasted that he'd put insects in the prison soup, but he was a prick, nerves shattered by an explosion when he was a soldier in Northern Ireland. He couldn't look me in the eye, dropping fags all over the place when I pulled him.

'I'll be honest wi' ye,' I said. 'If I don't get my tools tomorrow, one of you'll lose yer eye. Might be ye, might be ye, pal – nothin personal.'

'Whit! Ye're jokin'!'

'Naw, I'm no jokin'. So take yer fags an' beat it.'

I knew they would panic, that it would go right up the line. I was lying in my cell, reading a book, having a cup of tea, a bit of hash aside for the night, and they were all running about, panicking.

A couple of times I was so frustrated that I was close to taking a decision, throwing myself right into chaos, fuck everything. Jimmy helped me with that, too. I have to say that he gave me more sound advice in a short period than anyone had in my whole life. He used to say that I should expect to be kicked in the balls, that it would happen all through my life, but that what I had to do was weigh the consequences of my own response. In a flash, that advice would come back to me.

CHAPTER TWENTY-TWO

———————●———————

SHOTTS MAXIMUM-SECURITY Prison, 1991.

I had been due to go on a two-year release programme. After thirteen years I had finally been given a provisional release date. I was working at Edinburgh Zoo. A project had been designed for me to produce stone carvings of animals to assist the blind while under minimal supervision at the zoo.

Things had been going well until one day I was arrested by the Drug Squad. They had been tipped off by a screw, some slag climbing the career ladder. The Drug Squad dragged me off the street, searched me bodily and, when they discovered that I was clean, returned me to the prison later that night. Meanwhile, Fatty Pearce, the new number-one Governor at Saughton had ordered a cell search in my absence, breaching prison procedure.

During this period a number of screws had been bringing in dope for prisoners, cashing in on the arrests of major drug barons who had money to pay for drugs. When they were caught they blamed their behaviour on the pressures of working in a prison, the usual crap about a drug dealer leaning on them or the nervous disposition that had been brought on with the pressure of working with evil prisoners.

With my reputation I would have made a good catch. They had a problem with corruption, so it was no coincidence that I had been arrested. I had a public profile and would make good headlines as the mastermind behind it all. Those poor prison officers!

Fatty hadn't banked on the Drug Squad bringing me back, so he had me downgraded to a maximum-security prison. The grounds? A photograph depicting me in a public bar – hardly reason to deprive me of release and impose maximum-security conditions on me. He splattered me all over one newspaper in particular as the society high-flier with women and power, living the good life. The fat prick heralded himself as the epitome of integrity: 'The prison system cannot be compromised by the likes of drug barons.'

They transferred me to Shotts in handcuffs and with a four-man escort – for a photograph!

Shotts was complete chaos, right round the clock. There was continual noise, endless shouting after lock-up, a constant cacophony. The policy here is control by appeasement: the prisoners do whatever they want so long as they don't assault the staff or destroy the building. There are stabbings, slashings, hostages, fires, smash-ups every single day. Prisoners are sharing needles: there is a high incidence of HIV positive. Meanwhile the Scottish Office has been telling the public that Shotts prison is a huge success, pretending that the fortune spent on this new model has been worthwhile. It is a fucking nightmare.

I've been transferred here to stab or be stabbed. They need me to really fuck up now to whitewash yet another incident – an inglorious blunder by yet another Governor scoring points for himself and the prison authorities. Shotts management tell me straight: 'Ye've been shafted. Saughton have overreacted. Ye should still be in Saughton.'

George Shearer, the ex-Unit chief, is now a Governor here. 'Listen, look after yerself by all means, just dae it behind closed doors. The staff here won't bother ye', so don't wind yerself up.

Come an' see me if ye need anythin', okay, and call yer ma. She'll be worryin' herself sick.'

Malky McKenzie is here too. He is furious. 'Collie! Whit the fuck are you daein' here? Fuck! Waken yerself up, man. A maximum-security jail?' Malky gives me snout. 'Here's tobacco for ye. Nae doubt some cunt will gie ye a nightcap, there's loads a hash in here, but don't jag or powder yer nose 'cos the place is riddled wi' Aids.'

Davy McCallum's here too. It's more like the Unit than the Unit was. 'Hello, son! Have ye phoned yer ma yet? Tell her I was askin' for her.'

Shearer needs a favour. 'One of yer pals is here. He's on a second lifer fer shootin' somebidy in Glesga. Aye, that's right, it's Rab Smith.' Shearer tells me that someone has put it in Rab's head that if he stabs a screw, he'll be sent to the Special Unit. 'See if ye can put him right, will ye?'

Rab Smith? They put me next door to him. He looks mad with the long beard. 'Rab! How ye daein', man?' We're laughing together. I look him in the eye: 'By the way, ye grassed, ya cunt. Oh, aye, those fuckin' candles in the chapel. You told the priest it wis me, ya fuckin' real yin ye!' I couldn't wait to blether with him. He was one of my best pals, one of the old team, the Shamrock. I felt relieved to see him, someone I could trust, thank fuck, a pal.

We didn't work, just walked up and down outside our cells all day, drinking mugs of tea, reminiscing about the old days, wondering how things had happened – I mean, we had been altar boys together for fuck's sake! How had it all gone so wrong for us two especially? We had killed three people, so what had happened?

'Here, Rab. Whit's aw this aboot gaun tae the Unit? Are ye aff yer fuckin' heid? That mob'll try tae dae ye in for a start, an' anyway ye're no guaranteed tae get there, so don't kid yerself.'

He couldn't explain, couldn't express his desperation, just couldn't find the words: 'Saughton suited me, Shug. Ah'd've settled there. That's where Ah'd done ma last sentence, but the fat bastard fired me up tae Peterhead.'

Rab had been working in the welders' shop at Saughton. There had been talk of an escape in the shop, and when a dummy gun had been found, welded under his bench, he was shipped out. As a result he had been kept in handcuffs in one of the new cages for a year at Peterhead. It later emerged that the gun had been made by a screw and planted in his workplace to put the then Governor, John Brownlea, under pressure to be more disciplinarian with prisoners and abandon Prison Department plans for the new Grand Design.

'Fatty Pierce replaced Brownlea, and that was it, Shug. Ach, ma heid's a bit done in, that's aw, so don't worry, okay?'

I spent a year with him. He had fired a gun in a bar; the trial judge had agreed that the gun had gone off by accident but that he had no alternative but to sentence him to a lifer.

Eventually Rab's recommended for the Special Unit without a screw being stabbed. He sees no future for himself, but with some encouragement he responds. The Shotts management was relieved, although he had begun to communicate with staff, his whole manner had begun to change, he had improved.

'You'll get help there, Rab. The place is geared for guys like you, so don't gi'e up hope. This is yer one chance.'

Rab's family had been told that he would be going to the Unit as soon as possible. I had been told that he was going. Screws had been told. Then, out of the blue, he was suddenly knocked back, and by a prisoner in the Special Unit, a guy who had done him a wrong in the past.

Rab took the news well: 'Shug, look, you get on wi' yer own thing. Ah'll be brand-new, okay, so don't worry. There's an old movie comin' on, so let's get good seats. Ah'll get the tea.'

● I had began to feel worn out by prison: no release date, no sign of a future. Fuck it, I decided. I stopped taking food and liquids. Two days passed before the fast became official. I'd called the 369 Gallery to speak to Caroline McNairn – I had met her at the gallery and had really liked her – and Andrew Brown. He had been introduced to me many years before at one of the arts festivals and had liked my work so much that he'd bought my drawings. They had been supporters for some time now and would have an idea how to publicize the hunger strike. Caroline was worried and assured me that she would do all that could be done to help.

Somehow I felt relieved. The pressure had gone. No fear of death. I hadn't really made a decision: I had surrendered myself. I hadn't the strength left to be bothered any more. I now felt that I had a degree of control, power over my own life. Little as it was, it was something that couldn't be taken away. They had lost their influence over me.

'What's this all about, Hugh?' Dr Andrew Coyle, the ex-priest, the new top Governor. I felt slightly embarrassed. What do I say without sounding over-dramatic: 'I'm going to kill myself, Governor'?

Rab looked like an altar boy again, his head bowed, his hands firmly clasped. I felt apologetic about the Governor's position but made my own clear – I want a release date and a transfer or I'll fast to the death. This wasn't a protest but simply a process. 'Ye know this is wrong, Governor. I shouldn't be in this place. Can ye blame me, honestly?'

Coyle agreed about my situation but said that he couldn't condone self-destruction.

'What about your mother? How will she feel?'

He discovered later how she felt.

'And how are you today, Mr Smith?'

I could have sworn that Rab had been about to genuflect. I'd been watching his face, that boyish smile with the twinkling blue eyes, a Catholic face. Coyle was still a priest to him, someone to respect. He was an honest enough guy, but his priesthood meant nothing to me. They discussed football before the Governor left.

'Well Robert, see if you can look after this man, will you?'

I wound Rab up: 'Ya crawlin' bastard. He didn't take me on: Coyle's a Celtic fan, one of the boys, and you can't argue with that.'

Coyle and Felix McMahon, a screw, had been the only two Catholics who had worked in the prison: there had been very few who had ever managed to work in the system at all, but things had changed in more recent times.

Six days later I began to spit up black bile and experience severe pains in my head: I'd had no idea that this would be so painful. The prison population threatened a mass protest if I was left to die: I was overwhelmed by their support, it meant a great deal to me. Chalky White, a screw, threw a Mars Bar into my cell, saying he wouldn't tell anyone. 'Shug, take a shower for the water. The IRA do that, it stops the dehydration.'

Seven days passed. The prison doctor told the press that I would be dead with the next forty-eight hours: 'Mr Collins is very ill.' The Scottish Office said something about going through proper procedures. What a fucking irony: proper procedures! My ma said that she wasn't able to watch me deteriorate any longer: she now supported my position to fast to the death. Maybe it was going that way now, who could tell?

Dr Coyle's face had been twitching: he was under extreme pressure to have this matter resolved. The press had been more sympathetic towards my case than had been expected. The Scottish Office had offered a deal – but first I had to come off the hunger strike.

Oh, sure, humiliate me publicly, then pull a stroke. They are trying to save face at my expense. I can see the move a mile away. They just can't accept the facts of my case and refuse to take the responsibility of having had me sent here in the first place. Fatty Pearce fucks up, and they close ranks, protecting their own. Well, fuck them, it is release papers or nothing, no fucking deals. 'Dr Coyle, I'm past that stage. No deals, okay? I hate those fuckin' people. Tell them that. I fuckin' hate them, every fuckin' one!'

The eighth day. I had been rushed to the prison hospital – apparently I had been slipping into a coma. All I could feel was the excruciating pain. I wanted to scream, scream for my mammy. Somebody please help me, find my ma. Shearer waved a paper before my eyes: the release papers had been signed by the Secretary of State. Thank God! Thank God it was over.

I called my ma to give her the news first, and then called the gallery to speak to Caroline. My voice sounded dry and cracked, but I told her that everything had worked out for the best.

CHAPTER TWENTY-THREE

●

THE NEW PRE-RELEASE policy allows me a seven-day home leave: after sixteen years the idea of celebrating Christmas with my family seems more of a sentimental notion than anything else. I just don't know how I feel any more.

'Collins. Here's your licence, travel warrant and forty quid for your keep outside.'

The very idea of someone like me being allowed home on leave is really upsetting this guy. My ma knows I'll be home at some point, but I'll look in first at the 369 Gallery. Andrew Brown, the director, has supported my work all these years, and maybe I'll see Caroline McNairn. She had seemed worried when I was on the hunger strike, so maybe she's interested, maybe she fancies me . . .

Travelling's an ordeal, even walking along a street is a nightmare. Princess Street seems endless. I feel uncomfortable in my coat, it's like a copper's trench-coat. People keep walking into each other, it gets on my nerves. I'm on my way, however: I've stopped sweating and my breathing is becoming more regular, but my hands are still trembling.

Andrew and Caroline are in the boardroom as I come through the main door. I feel that something's wrong, although they try to put on a front. Caroline's avoiding my eyes, probably because she has no make-up on, and immediately disappears when I ask her to have a drink. Andrew's too busy but suggests some other time. My nerves are all over the place, although on the surface I'm doing my best to look cool, asking questions about how things are in the gallery. I don't hear the answers: traffic noises from outside the window are screeching through my brain, book covers are jumping at me from every shelf.

Thankfully, Caroline reappears, wearing make-up. She's looking cute, more composed and eager to leave the gallery. I feel comfortable in her company as we enter a bar, but for some reason I can't stop talking. She asks lots of awkward questions about my relationships with other women, and although I'm trying to be super-cool I find myself telling her everything. I can't believe it when she agrees to see me on my next weekend home leave. The trip to Glasgow becomes a blur of fantasies until the reality of the situation hits me. What if we sleep together? What if I can't get a hard-on? What if . . . ? What if . . . ?

I had bought some presents to take home and enjoyed opening them at night with my family, but the flat, the furniture, the very atmosphere seemed to be creeping up on me. It's twenty storeys up in a Cowcaddens high-rise, and it is giving me the fucking horrors. My brain seems to be moving around in my skull of its own accord, it's a weird sensation. Ornaments, too, are swaying with the building. Massive, useless objects constantly get in my way. Every time I turn around I knock something over. I begin to feel trapped, boxed in with furniture.

My ma wanted to avoid making any fuss, but her efforts to create an atmosphere of normality aren't working. I become convinced that they're all talking about me whenever I leave the room, falling silent again when I come back. I'll sound crazy if I ask them, 'You're all talking about me when I leave the room, aren't you?' I know they aren't talking about me, but I can't help the feeling that they are. I decide to have a bath: the bath is small compared to the prison's. There's a wire rack across the bath, holding soap, sponges, plastic bottles, face-cloths. I'm trying not to disturb anything, but I'm knocking things all over the place; when I pick one thing up something else goes until eventually I slip in the water and knock the whole lot over the floor. The bath is full of bottles bobbing around, and the water's everywhere. I leap out, grab my clothes and walk straight into a cupboard full of linen. Where the fuck's the front door? I pull on my clothes, run out of the house and head straight for the flat.

●   Kay Carmichael has left me the keys of her flat in case I need space on my own. It's in the West End. The flat's quiet and comfortable and not so high. There's a telephone. Should I call someone? I may have to go out if I do, and the thought of those streets . . . Will I call a bird? I might not be able to get rid of her afterwards. I should have sex, but what if I can't? What if I'm too wound up? What if I'm . . .

I remember the smack in my pocket. Someone gave it to me as a square-up, four grammes. I put a line out to powder my nose and feel the heroin running down the back of my nose, down into my throat. Good, it doesn't smell of shit. I hate people who hide their gear up their arses, the taste makes you immediately vomit and spoils the effect. I'm feeling better already. I make myself a coffee to bring it on and sit looking out the window into Kelvingrove Park. I wonder what's happening in the jail. Nine thirty: they'll all be locked up by now, lying in bed with a porn mag, wanking themselves. I like this flat, it's like being out. Fuck, I am out! I can do whatever I want, whenever I want: I can cook, have a bath, have a sleep, see people, go out, come in, anything at all. This is brilliant: this is what it's all about, being out in the real world, being a free man.

This smack is good kit. I wonder who brought it in. He must have kept the parcel in his mouth or just bluffed the search with it in his hand. All that other carry-on, shoving it up your arsehole in front of visitors. What do their people think of them when they do that? Then they actually deny that they wank themselves. It's crazy! Masturbate? Me? I'm a man! I don't do that! I'm not a wanker. Prison's full of headcases like that, people who become indignant if asked what they do at night or are accused of something trivial. I'm a murderer but I'm not a liar!

Well, anyway, I'll have a stronger line this time, there's plenty, maybe I'll chase the dragon or just smoke some in a couple of joints. Auld Cathy, my wee maw, the image of her fades. I wish she could see me now outside. Albert hated me smoking – he'd hate this. All he ever wanted to do was train, the mad bastard. I wonder what he's doing. Jack told me that he's changed, that he's a totally different guy, doing marathon runs for handicapped children and all sorts of other things for people. What the fuck happened, then? Why did this all have to happen if he ends up changed? Was there an inevitability to the murder or am I just a fucking nutcase who wanted to kill? Albert changed? That's hard to believe. Fuck, I've had nightmares about him for sixteen years, and now people tell me that he's a different guy, that he has really changed.

It's dark outside. It would be good to go for a walk in the park. No, I'd probably be lifted by the coppers if I'm out at night in a quiet area. They'd think I was a house-breaker or a car thief and then find out that I was a lifer. No, I'll have one more line and a joint. I wish I could stop scratching myself, this stuff always makes me itchy, especially my nose, it ends up looking like a strawberry. I love a good scratch coming out of a gouch, though: gouching's a real pleasure, just nodding off into quiet dreaming. My whole being slips into numbness, relaxes with the rhythm of my breathing, sinking deeper and deeper into its warm pool, free from the nagging urge to be doing something – just to be still, in absolute stillness.

God, I feel stiff. I must have nodded off, the television's still on and it's light outside. I'll go out for cigarettes, the walk will do me good. I love being out when it's very early, few people are about at dawn. I'll have a shave and a bath when I come back and make a good breakfast of fried bacon and eggs. They'll be getting the usual burnt offering at the prison, poor bastards.

The sky is light, some shadowy clouds, the ground glistening. Fresh air. I hear my own footsteps, walking briskly in the slight chill, echoing in the deserted street. I can run. Just run along the street, feel the air in my lungs. I feel like shouting, laughing out loud, shaking hands with someone passing. 'Mornin' there,' he says, a stranger. I try to pretend that I'm going to work. 'Aye, mornin', mate.' I feel wonderful, just to greet someone, a complete stranger. The Pakistani shop is open: I enjoy the light-hearted acknowledgements, just mindless chatter, nothing more, no intense questions: 'How are you? How do you feel?' Then all the advice that follows: how I must behave, how I must keep sculpting, how I mustn't let anyone down. All I want to do is get out. Be on my own without having to talk to anyone, without having to put on appearances for other people. People are a fucking nightmare. It's always the same thing: Jimmy does this, Jimmy does that, Jimmy wouldn't do that. I am not Jimmy fucking Boyle!

I've wound myself up thinking about it. I'll have a seat in the park for a while. Friends, they mean well, but they piss me off too. I need time on my own, some space. This is a nice park. I like the trees against the light-grey sky. The chill is nice too. That dungeon they had me in all those years ago, how did I ever get out of there? I wonder if they still use it? I love this breeze. I can feel it on my face but not through my coat. God, those suits I used to wear before I got done, trying to look like a gangster, trying to look like my da. All those years wasted, just to look like a gangster, and yet here I am now sitting in a park, looking at the sky and listening to birds. Have I really changed? Or am I just getting old? Is that all it is? Is forty-one old? This is depressing.

● This is better: a hot bath and a good shave. I'll give my ma a call later and go up about tea-time. She might tipple that I'm full of smack but I'll wear my glasses. Jim always tries to check my pupils, it really annoys me. The smack cuts out the stress, makes talking to people much easier. I'm not jagging, so what's the big deal? They all drink, don't they? Half the world is on something, they're all fucking high, so what's the big fucking deal with me?

Oh, no! My ma's made a huge tea! They get bigger every time I come home. She's asking questions while she's getting ready to go out: 'Did you sleep okay, Hughie? Did Kay phone? Mind and thank her now, son.' Jim's peering at my eyes, pretending to straighten my tie. The atmosphere's pleasant though. 'Jim, where's the hairbrush? Alec, mind and lock all the doors. Have you got your keys?' Alec's always brooding. I feel anger in him just below the surface, ready to explode. It's always tense, trying to talk to him, sort of forced, and yet he's my brother. He's a nice guy and never been in trouble. Am I just too fucked-up?

My ma's ready to go now and she looks stunning. She's into her sixties and is still very attractive with those clear, intelligent eyes. Jim's asking how it feels. How does what feel? He's younger than my ma: a good guy, looks after her. She doesn't let him mess her around. I wonder if they have sex. I'm enjoying being out. Aye, Jim. I feel good. The smack is making me chatty and humorous. Wee Betty takes my arm going down the road. The streets are slippery with black ice. My poor ma: the last time we walked down a dark street together she was trying to find a bed, and I was wrapped up in her arms. She's stood by me these past sixteen years, and never missed a visit. I wonder when she'll die? I hope I die first. I don't want to go through all that.

We're here now, at the pub where she used to work. It's a dive, a workmen's bar with a lounge. The manageress is an ex-copper, she helps ex-offenders. I'd fuck her: she has a nice pair of legs. Betty is showing me off: 'This is my eldest boy.'

People know about me, they shake my hand.

'This you out, son? Here's a few quid.' There's always a few quid, a wee bung. People do this when guys are just out of prison: 'Here, that'll get ye a drink.'

Blaring music, bright lights, loud, noisy voices. I can't take my eyes off the women: mini-skirted legs everywhere, the smell of cheap perfume, women laughing sexily with bright-red lipstick. I want to fuck them all. Thick mascara, tight skirts and high heels, flashes of knickers between crossed legs, tight, firm arses. God, this is torture: I can't stop looking at them. Men are getting on my nerves: their voices are irritating, talking about my old man, about his pals, that whole world. 'Aye, Hughie, I know your da.'

All the same old stories are starting over again, it's always the same speels.

'Aye, when he got the ten years . . .'

'Do ye remember Big So-and-so . . . ?'

'. . . Wee So-and-so, done a five in Peterhead? Aye, ye'll remember him. His brother done six.'

'How's yer da? Are ye going over to see him?'

'Big So-and-so just got done. He's in real trouble this time.'

The voices are coming out of the side of their faces, going on and on in this monologue.

'Big Collie Beattie? A fuckin' gentleman.'

'The Big Yin – bought me a half the other night.'

'Aye, I was out with him last week.'

Everybody in Glasgow was with Collie Beattie last week or with Arthur Thomson. Big Collie's and Arthur Thomson's social life must be exhausting. And let's not forget Jimmy Boyle.

'What's Jimmy doin' these days? Tell him I was askin' for him. He'll remember me from school. Just say Wee Sammy was askin' for him, he'll know right away who ye mean.'

Well, at least he wasn't with him last week.

I'm also identified, to a degree, by guys my own age. 'Aye, Shug, ye remember me don't ye? We used to drink together, before ye got done, in the Lunar Seven.'

I'm pretending to know them all, the ones who say they know me. Oh, sure. I'm terrible with faces, but I remember now.

I just want to talk to the women all night: I love their voices, their smells, mixed with alcohol. When one puts her hand on my thigh it sends a current through me like a cheap thrill. She's about forty-five, black hair, nice face, soft body in a tight black mini-skirt, black nylon legs. I can almost feel my dick inside her, every look she gives me is pure sex. I'll catch her later. These pints are making me piss all the time. I'll powder my nose while I'm in the toilet.

God, I need this line. I'll just sit here for a few minutes, let the smack take its course. Fuck, what a place. I think I'll just go back to the flat and have a few joints. Fuck the women, I'll just get stoned. I'd have to talk to them in the morning. I've only one more day left anyway, and then it's back to the nick. Big Martin will be missing me, being left on his own. He'll probably push me with the training; still, I enjoy doing t'ai chi.

Those two guys outside the cubicle are in love.

'Aye, Tam, ye're a good cunt. Ye're ma' best pal, an' ye know Ah'm yer best mate, eh, right? Whit? Whiddye say there, Tam? Mo Johnstone? Aw, here, whit aboot that goal, eh? Noo, wis that no a fuckin' belter, eh, mate? Whit? Whiddye say there, mate? Aye, me an' you, Tam. We'll show aw these fuckin' bams, eh? Jist me an' you, big man, eh . . .'

Me and you, eh? I bet they end up fighting when the boozer shuts.

My ma's suggesting that I go over to see my old man tomorrow. I don't want to go, I won't know what to say to him. I don't know if I want to say anything to him, I mean why should I?

'He's still your da, Hughie.'

They're both looking at me.

'Just go over, Hughie. He'll be okay with you. He was asking about you the other day.'

He's old now, sixty-odds. I wonder what he looks like. It's been almost ten years since we've spoken. God, I hope there is no animosity – the last time we spoke on the phone he told me to fuck off.

He had brought a parcel of drugs to the Unit: visitors were able to pass through without being searched in those days. I had promised to pass them over to the main halls through a contact of Davy Cochrane, a prisoner at the Special Unit.

Davy, however, fucked up – he opened the parcel and took a bit of hash with the intention of replacing it the following day, but he didn't tell me that the parcel had yet to be passed on. So I told my da that the parcel had been delivered, and people became alarmed when it hadn't been received at the destination. The guy who was to have delivered the stuff was threatened by a few heavies.

My da then appeared with some other guys at the Unit and, as expected, I was blamed for the whole thing: 'Ye nearly got a guy's eye taken oot, ya fuckin' rat, ye.'

Nearly ten years have passed since then. I wonder if he still has this on his mind. My ma has never been told why we fell out. But it has bothered me, especially when people have asked how he was getting on – it has made me feel guilty.

My ma wants me to go home with them: they might smoke a joint with me, so I'll go back up the road with them, and then get a taxi later to the flat.

'Imagine there's no heaven . . .'

John Lennon. She loves John and Yoko. She's playing a video of their last concert together: 'What a shame, Hughie. That poor guy never harmed anyone and look what they done to him, the bastards.' Betty launches into her favourite subject, politics and socialism. I'm telling funny stories about the Unit days. We're all in hysterics. Part of me wants to hug her, but I can't make the move. Maybe that's just the way all men are; who really knows?

'I'm heading off now, ma. I'll go over and see my old man in the morning and come back up later for my tea. There'll be nothing to eat back at the jail.'

'Right then, son. Mind and see yer da, okay?'

'Take care going up that road, son. You know what it's like this time of night.'

● The taxi driver's chatting as we reach Buchanan Street. I'm across the road from the Lunar Seven: sixteen years on and it's much the same. Will I go in for a pint? No, someone might recognize me. The place looks different from the image in my head, but the street is as busy as it was then. Where's the lane where I dumped the blade? Blades, God, I've had blades throughout my life. I'd probably feel more secure with one on me now, but the danger is that I'd use it. I remember standing over Mooney at that door. I must have come over in this direction – yes, that's right, into that fish-and-chip shop. Fuck, I had blood all over me from head to toe. I never thought I'd see this place again, it all seems a million years ago now. Jesus, I killed a guy at that door. I stabbed someone to death on that spot. Mooney's face: he was looking straight at me as he died. I wonder if he knew he was dying? What did he feel? Was he angry about dying? I remember the sick feeling in my guts when the reality hit me: the horror of killing him, the actuality of killing. I felt like a monster, like a fucking animal. What do I feel, now, honestly? I don't feel sorry for Wullie Mooney. I don't feel apologetic about what happened. I know that I'd do it again and that I'm still capable of that violence. Mooney had a blade that night but he didn't know what hit him: he was as helpless as a baby, even with his knife. He could have had a machine-gun and still wouldn't have stopped me – I was unstoppable, set to kill.

Murderer: I hate being called that but it's the truth – I am a murderer. I'm almost out now, I've done the time: why should I give two fucks? Why should I care about the past?

Sauchiehall Street hasn't changed, people milling around everywhere, heading for nightclubs. It's exciting. Glasgow's a violent city and probably always will be. I'm from the knife era but things are different – now it's guns and jellies.

*

● The flat's dark and cold. I put on the fire and television, roll some smack in a joint. I like having a bath completely stoned with a cup of tea and some biscuits, that's unadulterated pleasure for me. I love just lying here, dreaming. I'll have to finish that sculpture soon, the mother and child in granite. The big, worn-out face, it looks so sad with an arm around the baby. I've done well with this stone: working through the winter has put me ahead, but I'll be glad to have a break. The cold winds have battered me to the bone, and this arthritis is gradually crippling me. I'd better get out now, the water's cooling . . . Check those feet: I must have the ugliest feet in the world. Look at them, they're designed for climbing trees. I'll just lie here on the couch to dry. This stuff is heavy: I'll have to pack it in when I'm out. I'll get organized with a flat and things. Edinburgh seems a good place to live: I'd see Caroline. I dread all that carry-on, though, signing the dole, probation officers, trying to get train tickets, finding the right train, wondering where to get off. I hate looking stupid, having to ask people what to do. You get paranoid, ready to punch someone you think's staring at you. I'll do one more joint and get some sleep. I love that sky, deep, inky blue.

●

CHAPTER TWENTY-FOUR

TODAY I'LL HAVE to put on a suit: my da will be pissed off if I don't come up to scratch in front of his pals – I've no doubt I'll have to do the rounds with him. Why the hell am I doing this? He blanked me in the first place, and now I have to go through all this crap. I should never have let them talk me into it in the first place, but if I don't go, I'll never hear the end of it. I suppose I do want to see him but it's all the rest I resent, going to see his pals, when all I'd like to do is talk to him as my father. I don't know if that will ever happen.

The taxi driver is taking all the long roads. They all do it to up the fare. Well, there goes his tip. My hands are shaking. What am I going to say to him?

Possilpark, The Bronx, they call it, and no wonder. A drug dealer's haven. There are streets you just can't go into if you're a stranger. The police don't even go into some of the streets. I hate this fucking place. The guy next door to my old man has a pit bull, I'm told, a dealer no doubt. I'll kill the bastard if it comes near me, I hate those fucking dogs.

'Collins', here we are. When the door opens I'm surprised. He's obviously older, but healthier-looking, healthier than I've ever seen him. That powerful chest, and his scarred face: God, he looks battered. We both do, I suppose. The house is well furnished: television, boxing tapes, video, not a thing out of place, a cell. He asks whether I want a cup of tea.

'How long is that you've done, Hughie?'

'Sixteen years, da.'

He knows what it's like but he can't imagine that length of time in jail. We don't look at each other. He's talking all the time about things in the house, how they work and how much they cost. He reads a lot, too.

I'm doing the same thing, asking the obvious questions.

'How's Wee Ginger, da? Is Bates still alive? What about Collie?'

The conversation is forced, strained almost.

He shows me his new clothes, a wardrobe full of expensive suits, coats and shirts. He hands me thirty quid and calls for a taxi. Thank God, we're going out.

The room has ornaments everywhere, books piled up by the settee. He hires a woman to do his cleaning.

He comes back in, immaculately dressed in a suit and an expensive camel-hair coat: short, iron-grey hair, powerful build, he looks the part of a gangster. We're heading for the Gorbals. He doesn't speak in the taxi, just stares straight ahead. The last time I saw him like this was at a funeral. I know not to say a word: you never know who's listening. We arrive at the bar and I have an orange juice: I know he hates drink now, changed days. There's no name-dropping in this pub. Tam McMenemy offers me cocaine: 'No, Tam, but thanks.' (My da would be offended if I accepted drugs or money. I have to pretend that I don't need anything.)

The conversation is light-hearted. They can't believe how long I've been inside: they've all done time, but not a full sixteen years. Tam recalls an occasion when we met in jail. (A year later he throws himself off a veranda, twelve stories up, and dies.)

We go to another bar and meet more people, then another and another. Always the same routine. How long have you been in? Do you want speed? Hash? Pills? Always I say, no, thanks. My da gets me a taxi. I tell him I'll send a visit pass and arrange to see him again. There are no hugs, no handshakes, no contact at all, just 'Okay, I'll see ye then.' Still it wasn't so bad. Maybe things will improve with time.

My ma's furious.

'Thirty quid? And the money he spends on taxis, too!'

'Look, ma, I went over, okay? He can't say that I blanked him this time.'

'That miserable swine. He gives more to his pals for drink!'

Here comes another of those huge meals again. Alec still seems humourless but not tense, the pressures of studying for exams. I'm relaxed with them. The television's a good distraction. My ma won't let me do anything like help in the kitchen.

'Right, Hughie, out! Go and watch the telly. Jim, put on a video for Hughie.'

We watch the film *Highlander*. I like Sean Connery. Caroline's met him. I saw them in a photo together at the 369 Gallery.

I want out, back to the flat. All the activity is too much for me, and the continual questions about my da, about getting out, about how I'm feeling. Finally I'm leaving, hugging them all. My ma's close to tears: she keeps looking at me as though this is the last time she'll see me.

The quiet of the flat is a relief. People's faces fill my head: my da, just staring ahead, my ma looking at me that way, all those smiling mouths. My head's bursting. I strip off and pour out the rest of the smack. I feel tears in my eyes, then the rage squeezing its way up out of my face – I don't know why. Concentrate, concentrate on something, any fucking thing. I snort a line and begin t'ai chi. I dance naked, doing the slow, deliberate movements. Good old smack, you never fail. I keep dancing until the warmth floods through my brain. I dance slowly, deliberately, precisely, dance in the darkness of the room. I'll be glad when I fucking die, fucking glad to be free of all this bullshit.

This could be a room, a cell or a cave, who cares? I could do the whole lot of this smack, get it over with. Am I too scared? I put out one long line, enough to put me in a coma: one snort and that's it. What if I panic and try to call someone? All the embarrassment afterwards. No, fuck that. Am I really just scared of death? It's going to happen one way or the other, so what's the difference?

Sixteen fucking years – that's the difference. I don't want those bastards laughing. Big Martin: I wonder how he is? I wonder how they all are, all my pals? Jesus, I'll be glad to get back, see all their daft faces. I'll be glad to get back on the stone and get working again. Fuck all this socializing, it's all bollocks. I'll be glad to shut the door and have peace to think. I've enjoyed some of this, though. I should have gone out more.

● The journey on the train back to Edinburgh's not so bad. At least I have a window to look out of: no faces staring back at me.

Well, that's it.

At the prison I look at their faces, fucking screws. They hate the idea that I've been out.

'Wait in there, Collins.'

The visitors' waiting room. Women sitting around with kids: they'll find themselves here too, these kids have no chance. Hope they don't think I'm a screw. The reception screw collects me and takes me to be searched. I'm put in the Dog Box: the dirty walls, the smell of stinking sweat, the passmen trying to look above it all, ex-lawyers and fraudsters, white-collar workers, pricks.

'Right, strip off.'

The search is brief. I turn around, naked. They look in my pockets. I put on the prison gear – it's more familiar than my own clothes. Walking over to the hall, I pass a few guys going for visits. We exchange greetings. The hall throws me as I walk in: somehow it looks different, like the bowels of a huge ship. The roof is so high, and all those steel doors, row upon row, people locked behind them, it's a frightening place. The screws stand in groups and stare at me. I climb the stairs to the top landing and walk along the narrow passage: glaring lights on yellow paint, I hate that fucking paint. What the fuck's he smiling at? I step inside and am immediately struck by the bareness of the cell: a bed and a chair. There's no sign of life. Bang! The door slamming startles me: for a single moment I panic. I'm locked in – I'm locked in a fucking cell. This is prison. Where have those five days gone? I want out but I am confined.

For a few days I share lies with other guys, telling them how wonderful it was being out, how brilliant I was in bed. Birds? Fuck! I had a different one every night! My legs are like rubber!

I slide straight into the same old bullshit with very few problems, exaggerating the stories each time they are told. I have vague images of the five days, but that doesn't matter so long as I enjoyed myself. I'm convincing myself that I enjoyed the time outside – but did I? I feel that I've had a holiday but this is more real; this is where I have lived for so long, and still live, with my pals. I think I've come to enjoy this, enjoy or accept being in prison, going out on my little excursions and coming back to the security of prison.

My old man. How do I feel about him? He's much older now. I think he blames himself for all this. Do I blame him? The truth is that I have no regrets. Blame is simply a hollow, meaningless word. I'll have to give him a call to arrange a visit before the release. Yes, that would put things right between us again after all this time and let him visit me in jail too. He'd appreciate that – coming to see his boy.

'Hello, da? Is that you? Hughie here. Listen, I'm send—'

'Fuck off!'

'What? What the fuck's this?'

When the telephone slams down I feel jarred to the bone. I don't know what's happened. What the fuck's wrong? I call my ma to find out if she knows anything.

'Hughie, he says ye stole a wee bag a speed frae his pocket, son. Did ye leave the livin' room or somethin' like that? Did he leave ye on yer own at any time? Ah don't think he can face ye, tae be perfectly honest, Hughie. The best thing tae dae is jist forget him.'

I feel filled with rage: I'm deeply wounded and shaken by the tone of his anger. Why didn't he ask instead of making a blatant accusation? He just jumped to conclusions without a thought about my feelings. The dirty bastard.

'Hello? Don't hang up. Listen, I never touched yer fuckin' stuff. Ye'll never see me again after this, ya dirty fuckin' midden!'

'Aye? Good! Good! That's fuckin' great! Suits me, ya' fuckin' rat! Ye'r nothin' but a fuckin'—'

I slam the telephone down this time. The act brings me immediate gratification. Fuck him!

● I'm standing behind the gates, feeling dwarfed and nervous. I'm in the midst of screws exchanging duties. I sense their resentful looks towards me. I'm terrified that they'll pull me back, that something will go wrong, but just stare ahead. Isn't that what all hard men do? Isn't that what my da would do?

I wonder if he'll be out there waiting for me?

The face pressed against mine is familiar, but I just blank him and keep staring ahead. He's just another screw, a nothing.

'Right! Name and number, arsehole!'

Don't look back, they say: prisoners say that if you look back, you'll never leave the prison. Well, I'm looking back: the past looking back, looking back at two previous lives. The two previous lives are gone, they exist only in writing now.

Will he be there, I wonder?

The huge gate swings open to an oval-shaped blue sky. One step forward takes me through the present into the first two seconds of the future: the first second was the future, the second one is already the past.

Is this how he felt, getting out?

My ma's arms are around me. Caroline, too, hugs me. Alec's

smiling. Faces smiling at me. Can you imagine? Wham! The huge gate slams behind me. How do you feel, someone is asking.

How do I feel?

I want to say the right thing, something really profound, a speech about prison, about prisoners, about freedom. Those things you read about, see on newsreels.

How do I feel?

The flash is like lightning, the third second passes, the moment is gone and still moving. What did I feel? What do I feel? There is no answer.

'My da no here, ma?'

All Pan Books are available at your local bookshop or newsagent, or can be ordered direct from the publisher. Indicate the number of copies required and fill in the form below.